A Chatham-Kent Tapestry

A CHATHAM-KENT TAPESTRY

A Visual History to 1950

JIM & LISA GILBERT

BIBLIOASIS
WINDSOR, ON

FIRST EDITION

Library and Archives Canada Cataloguing in Publication
Gilbert, Jim, 1950-, author
A Chatham-Kent tapestry : a visual history to 1950 / Jim Gilbert,
Lisa Gilbert.

ISBN 978-1-77196-300-8 (softcover)

1. Chatham (Ont.)--History. 2. Chatham-Kent (Ont.)--History.
3. Chatham (Ont.)--History--Pictorial works. 4. Chatham-Kent (Ont.)--
History--Pictorial works. I. Gilbert, Lisa, 1957-, author II. Title.

FC3099.C45G55 2018 971.3'33 C2018-905917-6

Edited by Sharon Hanna
Copy Edited by James Grainger
Cover Designed by Chris Andrechek
Typeset by Ellie Hastings

Published with the generous assistance of the Canada Council for the Arts, which last year invested $153 million to bring the arts to Canadians throughout the country, and the financial support of the Government of Canada. Biblioasis also acknowledges the support of the Ontario Arts Council (OAC), an agency of the Government of Ontario, which last year funded 1,709 individual artists and 1,078 organizations in 204 communities across Ontario, for a total of $52.1 million, and the contribution of the Government of Ontario through the Ontario Book Publishing Tax Credit and the Ontario Media Development Corporation.

PRINTED AND BOUND IN AMERICA

To Harrison,
because you are the future of the past

Contents

FOREWORD

What we know today as Chatham-Kent is a patchwork of many different towns, villages, and the rural spaces in between. The municipality is the artificial product of a provincial government that mandated its amalgamation twenty years ago. Before that it was Kent County, with ten townships surrounding the city of Chatham in the centre.

There have been endless arguments about the advisability of this single-tier government. That debate will probably continue far into the future. However, there is one undeniably good result of the amalgamation: people from one end of Chatham-Kent now have more reason than ever to visit, and learn about, the other. The entire region is now their home. As Jim is fond of saying, this home is the size of a small European country, so there is plenty of geography—and history—to see out there.

This is one of the reasons we compiled this visual history of Kent County: to record the stories that together make up the past of today's Chatham-Kent. This book, with photographs and illustrations dating from early settlement to 1950, is organized into five chapters, the first four of which divide the former county into northeast, northwest, southeast, and southwest, before ending with a final chapter on the city of Chatham. From Thamesville to Buxton, Morpeth to Wallaceburg, we hope that our local readers will discover a shared history.

Whether you are from our own municipality or not, we would encourage you to get out there and spend some time in the various regions we talk about in these pages. Some of the buildings shown in these pictures are still around; others, you will have to use your imagination to see. The people are mostly gone, but their descendants are sometimes still there, and they would love for you to poke around and maybe have a coffee in a local shop.

And then there is the landscape. While it might change in some small respects over the years, the land itself has essentially remained constant. We always find it interesting to take an old photograph back to the very spot where it was shot, and to compare the picture with what is there today. That cultural landscape—what man has wrought—is often quite different, and that difference speaks volumes about how we view our environment today and how our forbears did in the past. It is a little history lesson right there in front of you.

Because we're both former teachers, we like that idea of you learning, wherever and whenever it might be. But more importantly, we want you to enjoy the experience. Whether you do go and visit the places explored here or not, we hope you find many things in this book to wonder at, to be amused by, or to be affected by in any way. The past is an amazing place—come experience our corner of it.

Chatham-Kent's past is a rich tapestry of many people, places, and events that are woven together to make that single-tier municipality what it is today. We hope that magic shines through in this book.

—Jim and Lisa Gilbert

INTRODUCTION

Kent County—what we know today as Chatham-Kent, the single-tier municipality incorporated in 1998—dates back to the Constitution Act of 1791, which redrew colonial boundaries to form Upper and Lower Canada. This area became part of the District of Hesse in Upper Canada, comprising all of what now is southwestern Ontario. A year later, Kent County was first formed within the district for election and militia purposes. However, our history goes back much further than the first appearances of the county in government documents. Historians estimate that the first peoples came to this region as early as 12,000 years ago. For centuries before the British arrived, there had been many different groups, established in nations, who called this land home. This book, due to its photographic nature, is not a comprehensive record of Kent County's history. It does not do justice to the rich narratives of this region's First Nations, whose civilization thrived before European settlement.

Other voices that are often overlooked in the historic record of Kent are those of the French-Canadian occupation prior to 1791. Although these individuals settled only a small portion of the region—what is now Tilbury East Township and Dover Township—they were part of a larger settlement pattern centred on Fort Detroit, which was founded in 1701. By the 1760s, some settlers, who had come mainly from Quebec, were cultivating farms on the south shore of the Detroit River in what is now Essex County. By the 1780s, some of them were venturing north into Kent. People like Jean Baptiste Lacroix and Alexis Labutte, and as many as twenty-five others, were settled along 'La Tranche', the name the French gave to the Thames River before the first survey was done in 1793.

The first land grant in Kent County, however, belonged to an Oneida woman by the name of Sally Ainse—a remarkable woman born in 1728 along the banks of the Susquehanna River in the United States. By 1783, she had amassed enough of a fortune to purchase all the land along the north bank of the Thames River (or *Escunnisepi* to many Indigenous groups), from its mouth to the forks, which later became Chatham. However, when Alexander McKee, acting on behalf of the British colonial government, "purchased" the land that takes in most of what is now Kent County in 1790, he ignored the requests of the Chippewa to exclude the lands they had sold to Ainse from the agreement. In the end, she was cheated out of all of her land except one 200 acre parcel, in modern day Dover Township.

As a result of McKee's Purchase, surveyors now began to plot the area, beginning along the lower reaches of the Thames. One might wonder why they chose to start there, when it was so far from Newark [today, Niagara-on-the-Lake], then the capital of Upper Canada. The reason: the surveyors were based in Detroit, which was still in British hands and served as the first capital of Kent County. The mouth of the Thames was

This watercolour by Owen Staples in 1915 shows an early view of Chatham in 1854.

also the entry point to Kent at the time, as the waterways were the only viable transportation route. This explains why, in the first survey of the townsite of Chatham, the street on the west end of the survey was named First Street by Abraham Iredell, the surveyor who plotted the land in 1795. First Street all the way to Ninth Street was the extent of the first survey; those streets still exist in Chatham today.

The first official settlers, many of them United Empire Loyalists, followed the surveyors. Frederick Arnold, Daniel Field, Thomas McCrea, and Matthew and Isaac Dolsen were some of the first people to claim title to land along the Thames River. In fact, "Dolsen's"—the complex made up of a distillery, trading post, tavern, and dock that grew up around Matthew Dolsen's plot in Dover Township—became the unofficial capitol along the lower Thames in the days before Chatham existed on anything but paper. Grist mills were also established along the river, so that farmers would not have to go all the way to Detroit to have their grain ground into flour.

Two early group settlements are worthy of notice here. First, the Moravians and their Delaware brethren began a new mission called Fairfield in 1792, when they came to the Thames from Ohio, where ninety-six of their group, mainly Christianized Leni Lenape, an Indigenous group from the middle colonies, had been massacred by the American colonists. This settlement flourished throughout the 1790s and the early 1800s and, like Dolsen's, provided a haven to travellers for a night or two. The Moravians continued to expand their mission until it was burned by William Henry Harrison after the Battle of the Thames in October 1813.

The second group of settlers were brought to the region by Thomas Douglas, Lord Selkirk, who wanted to help Scottish Highlanders who'd been dispossessed of their lands by the Highland Clearances. The Highlanders arrived at a place they called Baldoon, along the Chenal Ecarte (Snye River) in northern Dover Township, in 1804. The settlement was badly managed, and the Scottish immigrants faced the same challenges as other settlers—disease from swampy conditions, isolation, and unfamiliarity with the land and the climate. Ultimately, the Baldoon settlement failed, but the surviving settlers became the early backbone of Wallaceburg.

So these first pioneers, and others like them along the north shore of Lake Erie, in the southern reaches of Kent, began to settle and clear their land, build roads, and, to the best of their abilities, prosper in their new lives. They were gradually doing so when war came to the Thames.

War between Britain and its former colony, the American states, began in June 1812, and men from the region served in the Kent militia unit throughout the war. The fighting itself did not reach Kent County until the following year. In September of 1813, Henry Procter, in charge at Fort Amherstburg, was forced to abandon the fort after the British navy was defeated at the Battle of Lake Erie. He was accompanied by a very reluctant Tecumseh, the Shawnee leader at the head of the Indian Confederacy, whose group had also been stationed around Amherstburg. This retreat was poorly organized. Pursued by a very aggressive American army under the command of William Henry Harrison, the soldiers were forced into battle unprepared. When the Battle of the Thames commenced on October 5, just downriver from the Moravian mission in present-day Zone Township, the British army lasted a few scant moments before deserting the field. Tecumseh's Confederacy warriors stayed longer, but when their leader was killed, they too left the field to the victorious Americans.

For the rest of the war this area was considered American territory, but it was never militarily occupied. When the war ended, in early 1815, the settlers were left to pick up the pieces. Economic stability would take years to return to the region, but in the meantime other immigrants were anxious to invade the virgin forest that blanketed so much of Kent. In the period from 1820 to 1850, townships that make up Kent were beginning to take their current forms. Plots along the waterways were the first to fill up, but gradually settlement moved inward. The Sydenham River, which before the war had not seen any settlement, began to fill up in the 1820s. The Talbot Road, supervised by Thomas Talbot in Elgin County, became an important early roadway and, in the years after the Rebellion of 1837, the Middle Road, also under Talbot's management, began to open up the interior of the townships south of the Thames River.

Two Black settlements were also founded during this time of expansion. Both provided havens for escaped slaves from the United States while also including free Blacks who emigrated to Canada to make a new life. The first to arrive was fugitive slave Josiah Henson, who set up the Dawn Settlement just outside what would become the town of Dresden. Henson used his reputation as the model for Harriet Beecher Stowe's "Uncle Tom" to garner attention and funds for his community. Ultimately though, the community died with him.

More longlasting was the Elgin Settlement, originally founded through the efforts of William King, a Methodist minister morally opposed to slavery. Through marriage, King unwillingly found himself the owner of some fourteen slaves. He brought them to freedom in Buxton, in central Raleigh Township, and encouraged them to become educated, self-supporting members of society. This they did incomparably. For example, their school developed such a good reputation that some white neighbours sent their children—an uncommon occurrence in a society that by no means welcomed Black families in its neighbourhoods. The Buxton community is still thriving today.

Chatham itself began to develop at this time. Before the 1820s, there were very few people living within the confines of the first town survey. But after the Rebellion of 1837, when the military came to town, and when travel both by road and by water was easier, settlers came to the townsite in greater numbers. At this time, in the 1840s and '50s, many Black men and women came to the village as well, making up one third of Chatham's population. They too had come to escape tyranny in the United States, and while they faced discrimination here, they managed, like the rest of the community, to find a better life for themselves.

However, the catalyst that made Chatham truly the capital of Kent was the railway. The Great Western Railway was the first rail line to come through Kent County; it arrived in 1854. The line entered Kent at Bothwell, the newly minted town created by George Brown of *Toronto Globe* fame. It travelled through Thamesville, the brand new village created by David Sherman, and then, crossing the river, to Chatham. West of Chatham, the rail line travelled south through the swamp that was North Raleigh and Tilbury East, and then on through Essex County. The railroad brought immediate benefits to every stop on the line, leading to increased trade and passenger traffic.

After this, railroad fever was on. Towns everywhere vied to become the next depot on the next railroad to come to the area. The Canada Southern travelled through the southern regions of Kent beginning in 1872, and was the making of such places as Highgate, Ridgetown, Cook's Corners (later Charing Cross), Merlin, and Tilbury. The Erie and Huron travelled in a north-south direction and helped develop Dresden and Blenheim, among other communities. The Canadian Pacific came in the late 1880s, and the Detroit River and Lake Erie in the 1890s. Also part of this movement was the local electric line, the Chatham, Wallaceburg and Lake Erie Railway.

The coming of the railroads ushered in a time of tremendous growth throughout Kent County. The period from 1850 to 1900 saw the rise of countless village communities, and the increased traffic with the outside world led to the development of many new industries. New agri-businesses sprang up in several places, like the Dominion Sugar Company in Wallace-

Alexander McTavish sits on a mower, pulled by horses, on his Botany Line farm, 1946.

burg, the British-Canadian Canning Company in Merlin, and the British Leaf Tobacco Company in Chatham. In Wheatley and elsewhere along the Lake Erie shore, fisheries benefited from prompt delivery of their product to their markets in bigger cities. Lumbering too benefited from the railways. Not so much for delivery of their product—they primarily used the rivers to transport their logs—but because the steam engines needed wood, and lots of it, to maintain their speed. The railroads would help to fuel the economy of Kent well into the twentieth century.

In the meantime, though, competition had arrived in the form of the motorcar. The automotive industry might have been focused in Detroit, but it had many connections in Kent County. Some of our best and brightest men found their calling working for Ford and his competitors in Detroit, and many others stayed here to develop their own motorcars. The most famous was the Gray family from Chatham, who had partnered with Dallas Dort from Flint, Michigan, to produce the Gray-Dort automobiles. But they weren't the only ones. The Chatham Motor Car was produced in the city for a short time and the Hudson Motor Company in Tilbury produced excellent automobiles in the 1930s and '40s. Most successful of all was the International Harvester Company, which took over the Chatham Wagonworks producing wagons, then trucks. The company became Chatham's most important employer for many years.

In the first half of the twentieth century, the automotive industry also provided many offshoot jobs for the people of Kent. The Canadian Top and Body Company in Tilbury and Dowsley Spring and Axle Company, which became Ontario Steel, in Chatham are but two early examples of car component manufacturers.

Economic development was also accelerated in the late nineteenth century by several schemes to help drain the swampy land near the Thames, in Dover, Raleigh, and Tilbury East Townships. The Martin and the Myers waterwheels helped to open up land in Dover, and the Pike and the Forbes schemes did the same for Raleigh and Tilbury East. As a result of these efforts, some of the best land in the country could now be worked as farms.

A cycle of boom-and-bust oil and gas discoveries was kicked off when Charles Tripp hit an oil gusher near Bothwell in 1863. That boom lasted only a few short years, but oil is still coming out of some of the wells around Bothwell today. Later, in the first decade of the new century, people began prospecting for oil in and around Tilbury and southern Raleigh Township. Though the oil usually ran out quickly, the more plentiful reserves of natural gas spurned a new industry when uses were found for the resource. Natural gas continues to be an important industry in Chatham-Kent.

And so Kent County faced the new twentieth century with bright prospects. The manufacturing industry, in its many different facets, was booming all around the county. Agriculture, the backbone of Kent County from the very beginning, was really only just hitting its stride. Fishing was a lucrative industry. And, last but certainly not least, the cultural and artistic elements in Kent were just beginning to mature. These were the days of Arthur Stringer, the prolific novelist from Chatham, and Jeanne Gordon, the singer from Wallaceburg, two pioneering artists who led the way for others from the region to bring the fruits of their creativity to the world.

Of course, we know what the new century had in store; the citizens of Kent County were not immune to the events that swept the twentieth century. In the First World War, we lost some of our brightest lights, and many families lost a treasured loved one. The same tragedies were repeated in the Second World War. The Depression tested our strength and resolve, but it also instilled a sense of community born of hardship. Like elsewhere, we emerged from that devastating first half of the century with the satisfaction of knowing that we had survived, while still retaining the sense of excitement for the future.

These early years of Kent County show that, like other places across the continent, we began by doing battle with the land, and wrested strength and prosperity from that task. We developed faith in the idea of progress, and used our spirit and ingenuity to seize what we could from it. And our county thrived. We did not stop too long to think of the consequences our headlong rush into modernity might bring. That was the task for the future.

GORE
NTH. BR. OF SYDENHAM R.
OTTER CR.
WALLACEBURG P.O.
KEITH P.O.
DRESDEN P.O.
ERIE & HURON RY.
OLDFIELD P.O
CHATHAM
LITTLE BEAR CR.
PRINCE ALBERT ROAD
ERIE AND HURON RY.
APPLEDORE P.O.
DARRELL P.O.
DAWN MILLS P.O.
GROVE MILLS P.O.
EAST BR. OF SYDENHAM RIV.
FLORENCE
DANTE P.O.
ZONE
CAMDEN
LOUISVILLE P.O.
THAMES RIVER
Con. A.
THAMESVILLE P.O.
GREAT WESTERN RY.
NORTHWOOD P.O
LOUISVILLE SIDING
ARNOLDS CR.
Con. B.
Gore
MORAVIANTOWN
Block Con.

CHAPTER ONE
Northeast Kent

When drawing the boundaries of northeast Kent for this book, we chose the land north of the Thames River and east of the city of Chatham. The dividing line with the northwest is the Dover-Chatham town line, or Highway 40. The northern boundary is Lambton County, where the Sydenham River flows through from east to west to empty into Lake St. Clair. Before 1998, the northeast consisted of the townships of Chatham, Camden, and Zone—including the gores that comprise the northern sections of both Chatham and Camden. In the earliest days of settlement, these gores were designated as part of Lambton County, but when Lambton formed as a separate municipal unit in 1850, the settlers pushed to be included in Kent County and those territories were added. The northeast is home to many populous communities rooted in some of the most important historical events in southwestern Ontario's history.

The northeast was first settled along its waterways, starting with the Thames River, and later, along the Sydenham. Frederick Arnold, who had settled along the south bank of the Thames in Howard, at Arnold's Creek, had four grown sons. Two of them—Lewis and John—chose to settle in Chatham Township, and Louisville is named after the first of them. Captain William Baker, who had settled further west near what would become the city of Chatham, received Crown property on the Thames in the northeast. It would pass into the hands of his daughter Anne, who married into the Eberts family, reminiscent of the community of that name. Further east, United Empire Loyalist Joshua Cornwall became the first settler in Camden Township, where he built a mill, which was burned down during the War of 1812. David Sherman, son of the pioneer Lemuel Sherman, originally platted the town that would later become Thamesville.

Settlement along the Sydenham began around 1820, in the Gore of Camden, in what was Lambton County at the time. Dawn Mills was the pre-eminent settlement in the early days, later to be eclipsed by Dresden, which was, for a brief time in the 1880s, the second most populous town in the county. That distinction was claimed by Wallaceburg, further west, in the Gore of Chatham Township, a distinction it maintains to this day.

Indian Zone Township was one of the smallest townships in Kent County, and one of the latest to be designated as a separate township, having been officially formed around 1850. Yet it was also the site of some of the county's most historical events: the founding of Fairfield by the Moravian missionaries and their Indigenous partners in 1792; the Battle of the Thames; the burning of Fairfield in 1813; and the founding of Bothwell by George Brown in the early 1850s. One cannot forget Bothwell's subsequent oil boom, one of the most spectacular in Canada. These events all happened in Zone Township.

The Moravian community moved across the river after the War of 1812, but another First Nations settlement remained in the area and still does today. Walpole Island is unceded Indigenous territory and actually consists of two islands, Walpole and St. Ann's, just across the 'Snye' (Chenail Ecarte, or narrow channel) from Chatham and Dover Township. The Indigenous people who make up the Walpole Island Nation include the Ojibwe, Potawatomi, and Odawa.

Patterns of settlement, which began along waterways, eventually moved inland. As roads improved, villages like Kent Bridge and Dresden became more prominent. Later, the railroad—the Great Western in the 1850s and the Erie and Huron in the 1880s—blazed its way through the northeast, boosting business and development in every settlement along the route. Eberts and Wabash are products of their proximity to the rail lines.

Another community worth highlighting is the Dawn Settlement, which represents one of the main strands in Kent County's history. Founded by Josiah Henson in the early 1840s in Dawn Township (later part of the Gore of Camden), the Dawn Settlement offered safe haven to Black refugees from slavery, allowing them not only to be free, but build lives for themselves as equal members of society. Henson himself escaped from Kentucky in the 1830s and made his way to Dawn Township, where he joined with abolitionists from Britain and Canada to form the Dawn Settlement on 200 acres of land near the Sydenham River. A year later, they established the British and American Institute, a vocational school for residents. While it endured its controversies, the Dawn Settlement allowed many Black refugees to become self-sufficient in their new lives in Upper Canada. While many returned to the United States following the Emancipation Proclamation in 1863 and end of the civil war two years later, a significant Black community remained near Dresden.

A yearly event that grew out of Josiah Henson's remarkable faith was the summer camp meetings that occurred near the institute. People, black and white, came from far and wide to hear Henson and other preachers speak. This was an early tourist attraction in the Dresden area.

Another major theme in the history of Kent is topography, specifically the need for drainage. The land in the northeast was not, in general, as swampy as Dover Township or Raleigh or Tilbury East, with the exception of the quadrant's northwest section. However, the land in the northeast, while very fertile, was also flat. Apart from the two rivers at its northern and southern reaches, there were only a few creeks, running east-west, mainly in the southern part of Chatham Township. Heavy rainfall would create pooling water, causing flooded crops. The early citizens of these townships, in particular Chatham, worked together to dig dredge cuts. The network of cuts and drains that they constructed, without the use of heavy machinery, is a testament to the foresight and work ethic of our forebears.

Better drainage meant that farmers could try new methods of farming or grow new crops. One of those new crops was sugar beets. Area farmers started growing sugar beets for factories in Michigan, which had been established to compete with the sugar-cane industry, which relied on product sourced from tropical climates. After a few years, industrialists and entrepreneurs realized that they too could cash in on this moneymaker. Factories soon opened up in Wallaceburg, Chatham, and Dresden (though the latter closed before it became profitable), providing a good living for workers and local beet farmers.

In general, what characterizes the northeast quadrant of old Kent County, as defined by this book, is the number of larger towns that have flourished here. The northeast is the most populous part of the region, outside the city of Chatham. These towns—Wallaceburg, Dresden, Thamesville, and Bothwell, as well as the smaller communities of Kent Bridge, Eberts, Louisville, and Wabash—have stood the test of time, and still thrive today within the greater Municipality of Chatham-Kent.

This sketch from the *Historical Atlas* published in 1881 shows the Joseph Montgomery home at Oungah, a small community at the crossroads of the Dover/Chatham townline (Hwy 40) and Concession 9 (Countryview Road). A well-established farm with a stately Victorian farmhouse, the property is still owned by the Montgomery family.

Even a small community like Louisville could muster twenty-six men for a gun club, pictured here, at the turn of the century. These men—many of them descendants of Kent pioneers who were subsistence hunters—were carrying on a way of life, even as surrounding woods and wildlife were fading.

George Brown, a Father of Confederation and founder of the *Toronto Globe*, also founded the town of Bothwell. He sponsored the first survey, and the town was built on his land. However, while George built this house on Chestnut Street, he never moved in—thanks to his wife, who refused to live in the 'backwoods.'

John Robinson and his son are seen here on an ornamental horse-drawn hearse, circa 1890s. As with most undertakers in the nineteenth century, John also made furniture and other carpentry, including this hand-crafted hearse. Eventually, John was trained in embalming, and later became one of the first Funeral Directors in Ontario. The Robinson name is still connected to funerals in Bothwell today.

After the Battle of the Thames, General Harrison marched his victorious Americans to Fairfield. Harrison was friendly at first, but when British General Procter's papers were discovered in a missionary's home, he determined to burn the village down. This 1838 painting by Lieutenant Philip John Bainbrigge looks across the river to the new settlement at Fairfield, rebuilt after the war.

While many believe that railroads spelled the end of stagecoaches, this photograph of the Bothwell and Florence stagecoach dates to 1908—almost fifty years after the railway came to town.

Whitebread, a tiny settlement in the extreme northwest corner of Chatham Gore, was so small it only had a train stop, not a station. The building pictured here was both a post office and a store where you could buy a train ticket, though you had to hail the approaching locomotive, as many students did to commute to school. The Whitebread settlement began with a Methodist church, which moved there in 1881 from Baldoon. It was named Whitebread after a Mr. William Whitebread, who had dug the drain that ran nearby on the county line.

On April 1, 1863, the famous Lick gusher (named for American speculator John Lick) started and the Bothwell oil boom was on. The population reached 7,000 and a forest of derricks littered the roads. In 1867, the speculators had left and a fire ripped through George and Main Streets, leaving Bothwell as if the boom had never happened.

One of the larger industries in Bothwell in the early twentieth century was the basket factory, in the days before cardboard and plastic overtook the packaging industry. Bob Tunks owned a factory that sported an assembly line, with tools all handmade by Bob, a blacksmith by trade. At peak times, it employed about 100 people.

Considering that the railroad tracks ran right next to The Brunswick House, it doesn't come as a surprise that there was almost always a hotel on this spot in Bothwell. The first hotel burned in the great conflagration of 1867. Brunswick was the last, until it too burned and was replaced by a creamery.

Bothwell's second public school on Queen Street served children south of the railroad tracks and on towards the Thames—land that was part of Bothwell until the town petitioned for a size reduction in 1905.

This playful portrait of an area family breaks the stereotype of the dour, unsmiling Victorians as they are seen in many photographs.

After the oil boom ended, Bothwell lost much of its population and its services—including the bank. In 1872, the town council commissioned the building of a multi-purpose structure on Main Street—including a town hall and fire department—in the hopes of attracting a bank. They didn't find a tenant for the main floor until 1905, when Merchants' Bank moved in. Eight years later, the bank bought the whole property for $2000 on the condition that council tear down the building seen here.

Main Street, Bothwell, circa 1910s. The Brunswick Hotel, a local landmark, has burned down. Roads are not paved, nor parking direction mandated, despite the presence of automobiles. A livery occupies the north end of the building at left. Bothwell, like many other towns, was on the cusp of modernity but still looked much like a rural nineteenth-century community.

The Joy House Theatre arrived in the late 1940s, to the delight of George Oliver, who had been appointed in 1947 by the Bothwell council to bring a movie house to town. With much prompting, he had convinced Harland Rankin, owner of the Centre Theatre in Chatham, and Vannie Chauvin, owner of the Plaza Theatre in Tilbury, to partner in the enterprise.

In 1894, the Bothwell Dairy Company was formed by John Labatt and T.D. Hodgen, the new owner of 1000 acres of grazing land just outside town. They set out to convince local farmers to buy dairy cattle and sell the milk to them, but instead, many people, like A.H. Reynolds (pictured here), formed their own small dairies to sell to Bothwell townfolk.

In the 1930s, Dr. Isabel Rendal Ralph purchased this house, built in 1906 by W.R. Hickey, to open a nursery for children with disabilities. She was more successful running Rosedale College, which held summer courses for female teachers. In 1950, Isabel departed suddenly for New York State to further her education in psychiatry. She returned sixteen years later to run the 1200-bed Cedar Springs Hospital—the first woman in Ontario to hold such a position.

These tennis courts were installed on land owned by John Puddicombe in 1896. A robust tennis club was formed for Bothwell gentlemen and their younger protégés. Also included on the lot were greens for bowling—another popular pastime.

In 1910, Dent Brothers, who also owned the town's hardware store, brought the first Ford dealership to Bothwell. To promote their cars, which were still a novelty, the Dents sponsored a "Ford Picnic" every year. A rally of vehicles, like those seen here, would gather on Main Street and motor to Rondeau Park, where lunch and ice cream were provided by the host.

After selling their first town hall to Merchants' Bank, the Bothwell city council set about constructing a new one on the corner of Main and Elm streets, as pictured here. Completed by 1916, the building also held the library, theatre, jail, and offices for public works, police, and fire. Today, the theatre is still in use, and the building is considered the heart of the community.

Like many towns, Bothwell was built and later flourished because of the railroad. The earliest businesses and industries were all clustered around the train depot, seen in this postcard from 1908, at the southern edge of town. George Brown, being at the centre of influence in Toronto in the 1850s, bought the land through which the Great Western Railroad would come.

Bothwell fire volunteers, 1940s. The town minutes reveal that council regularly replaced the clutch on the first motorized fire engine because none of the volunteers knew how to properly operate it. Other requests were to buy more firehose. Why? When a fire burned across the railway, firefighters were forced to lay their hose across the tracks, only to have it severed by a passing train.

Bothwell's first school burned down in the 1870s, but town council didn't build a new continuation school until 1885. Pictured here, the building housed a high school on the top floor, with elementary students on the first level. After the Second World War, high school students were bussed to Glencoe, and in 1950, a new elementary school was built.

In 1954, Donald and Trevor Rees decided to convert the old continuation school to the Glendale Candy Factory. Using the first floor, the staff of seven made more than thirty different candy products. Glendale was one of the last independent candy makers in Canada.

In 1854, a post office was established in Dresden to serve the town's 300 residents. After several moves, the brick post office depicted here was built at the corner of St. George and Main Streets in 1913. Initially the mail for Dawn Mills, Rutherford, and Dawn Valley was sent to Dresden, until local roads improved enough for rural delivery.

A bridge at Dawn Mills under construction, 1897. Here, workers prepare to lower a large stone from a wagon to build a solid southern foundation approach to a wooden bridge spanning the Sydenham. Ultimately, the wooden structure lasted only a short time—within twelve years, there were calls for a new iron bridge.

Bothwell's proximity to the Delaware Nation at Moraviantown has created strong ties between the two communities. Here, the No.3 Company, Moraviantown Contingent of the 26th Battalion is seen mustering in the town on June 14, 1907. First Nations men enlisted in the military in large numbers and distinguished themselves in both World Wars.

In the early days of Dresden, felled logs were skidded to the main trail, loaded onto sleighs, and then hauled to the river bank and piled. In spring, they were rolled into the Sydenham River and were floated down to the mills or loaded onto scows, as seen here, circa 1880s.

To earn a living, many early settlers took up positions on more established farms or hired themselves out as lumberjacks to area timber companies. The district around Dresden was covered with valuable trees such as maple, oak, elm, and walnut, including the logs pictured here, transported by Albert Stevens, circa 1900.

John Gordon's Stave Mill, circa 1900s. John Gordon established an industry making wooden staves for barrels on the north bank of the Sydenham River in an area later called Camden Street. These barrels were used to ship products like apples and whisky.

In 1873, Alexander McVean and H. Currie established a sawmill, pictured here, at the west end of Hughes Street in Dresden. Over the years, this mill manufactured hubs and spokes, hockey sticks, and baseball bats. It was eventually sold to the Kelsey-Hayes Wheel Company in 1928.

The Queens Hotel was located on the southeast corner of the Market Square in Dresden's early days. Later, the hotel moved to the southwest corner of St. George and Lindsley streets. On December 11, 1932, it caught fire, and although the Wallaceburg Fire Department was called to help, the once-beautiful Queens Hotel was reduced to rubble.

Here, workers Bill Ellis, Andrew Bear, Chris Brown, Art Hoyles, and Harry Bishop mix concrete for the laying of a sidewalk in front of the Bank of Commerce, 1904. The Dresden post office was situated in the rear of the bank. Postmaster John Watson is partially visible in the doorway, to the right.

Fishing in the Sydenham River, likely at the turn of the century.

W.H. Taylor and James Smith decided to build a mill on the Sydenham River, which led to the settling of Dawn Mills, named for what was then Dawn Township. By 1830, there were grist and sawmills. Soon after, they were joined by a general store, St. James Anglican Church and cemetery, several hotels, as well as a sawmill and woollen factory. As the years progressed, Dresden, some six miles downriver, began to grow while the once thriving Dawn Mills languished. By 1890, places like Prangley's Flour Mill, pictured here, were abandoned.

In 1889, the wooden bridge in Dresden was replaced with an iron one. The replacement cost $17,000 and used ballast stone from Scotland. The bridge was designed to swing open, from the centre, turned by a hand crank, for the passage of tall-masted river traffic.

When E.B. Madden bought R.P. Wright's grocery store at the corner of Brown and St. George Streets in Dresden, he convinced his son Jack to be the delivery boy by buying him a team of black ponies and a wagonette, made locally by the Rudd Carriage Factory, as seen in this photograph. Before this time, groceries were delivered in a single wheelbarrow.

Organized baseball in Dresden dates to May 15, 1890, when a junior boys club was formed. This undated postcard shows an early 1900s team, with all team members listed. Dresden succeeded in winning the Baseball Cup on July 1, 1915, outplaying the other seven teams in their league.

Noted Right House was the name of this early Dresden millinery and dry goods store, seen here in 1884. The owner, Alfred Grover, is standing at far right.

The life of Henry Weston, a retired riverboat captain, illustrates how Dresden residents adapted from river travel to rail. Weston would meet train arrivals on his omnibus pulled by "Old Joe," his faithful horse. The story has it that Old Joe fell ill and had to be shot. A few days later, Weston himself died—an event he had predicted years before.

As early as 1870, a vein of clay ideal for brick production was found in land north of the Sydenham River, less than a half mile west of the Dresden bridge. By 1875, the Henry Parks Tile Yard was located on that land, pictured here circa 1880. Four years later, bricks were in demand for home construction, selling for four dollars per thousand.

Built of brick in 1874, a year before this picture was taken, Dresden's town hall also featured a bell for the tower, donated by early town developer D.R. VanAllen. The lower floor included a town jail and a market for meats, produce, and livestock. The structure burned down in a spectacular manner in the early morning hours of March 18, 1942.

Norm Thomson, a talented First World War pilot, became chief engineer at Hayes Wheel and Forgings in Dresden. Thomson persuaded his manager, William Whistler, to manufacture a plane he had designed. Known as Valkyr 1, 2, and 3, the planes failed to find a commercial niche. Here, Norm Thomson (right) stands with his Valkyr 3 and his friend Lorne Stepper, circa 1930s. By 1939, the last Valkyr, which had been stored in Thomson's garage along with the plans, was lost to a fire.

In 1920, George Lawrence bought the McVean Mill, which had moved from Dawn Mills in 1867, to the south bank of the Sydenham River, east of the Dresden Bridge. George continued to operate it as the Dominion Milling Company—as seen in this postcard from the 1920s—until 1947, when it was sold to St. Clair Grain and Feeds.

The Union Block sat on the east side of St. George Street, between Queen and Main streets. In the early 1900s, most buildings were clapboard—including the Dresden Standard, seen in the foreground. On March 21, 1902, a fire wiped out the block, leading to new brick edifices.

Captain James Davidson agreed to establish a sugar beet factory in Dresden in the early 1900s, provided that the town offered financial incentives. However, a mistake on the legal documents gave a $20,000 tax levy (about $1700 a year) to the town rather than a fixed assessment of $20,000 payable to Dresden coffers each year. As a result, Davidson abandoned the massive structure, which included a five-storey building, outbuildings, and machinery on an eleven-acre lot—an investment of $600,000. By 1904, the date of this picture, he had moved the plant to the United States, leaving Dresden with the rusting remains of a once-promising industry.

Dresden's Main Street, 1907. At far left is the Westcott Hotel, with only one of its two distinctive towers visible. To the right is the Robert Aiken Dry Goods Store, then the E.M. Smith Woollen Store, draped with a banner reading: "Retirement from Business Sale with Wholesale Prices."

Reverend Josiah Henson fled slavery in Kentucky and successfully escaped to Canadian soil in 1830. With the help of the Society of Friends (Quakers), abolitionists from the northern states, and sympathizers from Great Britain, he fulfilled his utopian vision by purchasing 200 acres on the Sydenham River and opening a vocational school called the British-American Institute. The titular character in *Uncle Tom's Cabin* was inspired by Josiah. In 1947, William Chapple, a grandson of Dresden's first village clerk, restored Josiah Henson's home and conducted tours for many tourists coming to see "Uncle Tom's Cabin." The home is pictured here that same year, on the Chapple farm.

Josiah Henson passed away at the age of ninety-four in 1883. He was buried in the family plot a few yards away from his home just outside Dresden.

Brown Street, with newly completed Bank of Commerce, 1906. The *Dresden Times* building, J.W. Harris & Co. Undertakers and Furniture Makers, and the Westcott Hotel are also visible.

This photograph looks north towards the steel bridge, built in 1889 over the Sydenham, at the height of the 1904 flood. The flood tossed a sailing vessel, the *Vianna*, onto the river's bank; destroyed one million board feet of lumber and 7000 fence posts; and dumped a large amount of debris and silt over many homes in Dresden.

The Clifford Hotel was built on the site of an earlier hotel, the Shaw Hotel, around 1882. Seen here in 1905, the three-storey hotel featured balconies on each floor and a glassed-in turret, where a view of the town could be had.

This aerial view of Dresden reveals the beauty of the town and surrounding landscape, which vistors to the Clifford Hotel would have gotten a taste of from its glassed-in turret.

The flood of 1947 not only affected communities along the Thames River, but those along the Sydenham. Dresden was hard hit by flooding. Here, Mrs. Mary Jane Traxler, the oldest woman in Dresden, is rescued after being marooned in her house by fast-rising flood waters.

Even in the earliest days of settlement in Kent, men liked to get together to watch race horses. As time went on, the men were often joined by their families, who came to cheer the horses on. More recently, harness racing became a more established event in Dresden, and today you can legally bet on the horses. These pictures, taken from the *Chatham Daily News* in June 1946, show a crowd of people cheering on the sulkies at the Dresden Raceway.

This postcard shows the Robert Aikin store in 1909. One year later, downtown Christmas Eve shoppers were gathered at this spot watching a fire burn on the south side on Main Street. Two spectators, local businessman D.V. Hicks and Methodist minister Reverend George Long, were standing in front of the store when an explosion showered both men with bricks and debris. Hicks died almost immediately, while Long survived only a day.

The Florence String Band, early 1900s.

Originally known as Zone Mills, this community in northeast Zone Township changed its name to Florence in honour of Florence Nightingale, the famed Crimean War nurse. By 1869, the hamlet boasted 350 inhabitants, two hotels, a sawmill, and eventually, four Protestant churches and a weekly newspaper, the *Quill*. Unfortunately, the town suffered many fires. Downtown Florence, pictured here circa 1908, was almost totally wiped out in 1934—following blazes in 1858, 1881, 1905, and 1929.

In early days, the community of Kent Bridge, seen in these two photographs, was known as Kelley's Corners. The name was later changed to Gee's Ferry to recognize Christopher Gee, who ran a brick yard and ferry service. Gee is remembered for his attempt to construct a floating bridge by tying seven scows together. The first flood that came along destroyed the floating bridge. In 1854, Kent Bridge, an enclosed wooden toll bridge, was built, leading to the settlement's final name change in 1880.

Early settlers harvested the virgin forests that covered Kent County. Even in 1910, after a century of cutting down the trees, men were able to find logs like the ones seen in this picture from Dent's Sawmill, located in North Thamesville. Today, there is less than five percent tree cover in our municipality.

In 1904, a group of Kent Bridge farm boys formed a soccer team. Despite being underdogs, they won the Frederick Arnold Memorial Society Cup in 1906 and the Clements Cup Championship in 1907. From 1904-1907, they lost only one game against some of the best teams in Western Ontario. Shown in this 1907 picture, along with the team, are the cups they won, from left to right, the Dresden Cup, the Fleming Cup, and the Arnold Cup.

During the winter of 1915-16, recruitment began for the 186th (Kent) Battalion. During the First World War, this unit was based in Chatham, but it sought recruits from all over the county. Here, members of the battalion are transported near Thamesville in 1916. The 186th sailed to England in March of 1917, where it was broken up and absorbed into the 4th Reserve Battalion.

"There is a hotel on every corner," said one writer of Thamesville in 1900. The establishments included the Empire, opened in 1897 by the Bambridges, and the Tecumseh House, opened in 1900 by George Watts. These hotels flourished until the citizens of Thamesville voted to go "dry" in 1905.

On October 24, 1907, when Thamesville was a "dry" town, an accident on the Grand Trunk Railway (CNR) line in town jammed a car loaded with whisky. Several residents removed the "cold tea" and stored it in their cellars—under the spying eye of a reporter and his camera. As a result, seventeen men and boys were charged and brought to trial before Justice of the Peace William Ingalls.

A barn raising, like this one in Thamesville, was a common early practice and major part of community life for settlers, who could otherwise grow quite isolated.

The popular pastime of lawn bowling led to the creation of new businesses in Kent County. Louis Schmid (third from right), a Bavarian jeweller and clockmaker, was visiting Thamesville when he met John Duncan (far left). After bonding over their love of bowling, John gave Louis a deal on rent for his building next to the Post Office on Victoria Street. Mr. Schmid opened a jewellery store that remained an important business in Thamesville for eighty years.

In September 1911, the citizens of Thamesville, led by Katherine B. Coutts, erected this boulder at the site of the Battle of the Thames to commemorate the loss of Tecumseh. Today, this monument sits in a roadside park, just off the battle site.

Thamesville residents used to have two choices for rail travel: the Canadian National Railway, which still uses the line today, and the Canadian Pacific Railway, which had a station in North Thamesville, where Base Line meets Victoria Road (Hwy 21). Today, residents must go to Chatham to board the train that passes right through their town.

Wallace Leeson and Herson Miller, two entrepreneurs from Detroit who had perfected the process of rust-proofing steel wool, set up a business in Thamesville in 1933. They named it Bull Dog Steel Wool, and it remains today the only steel wool manufacturer in Canada.

"Down our main street came a procession…Marshal Foch, the two John Bulls, Uncle Sam, Gallant Little Belgium, the whole gang, dragging at a rope's end Deptford's own conception of the German Emperor…. Hang him they did." These are the words of noted Canadian writer Robertson Davies, describing the burning in effigy of the Kaiser at the end of the First World War in his novel *Fifth Business*. The book is the first of the Deptford trilogy, a fictionalized version of Thamesville, where Davies was born and grew up. This event forms a vivid episode in the early life of Dunstan Ramsay, the protagonist.

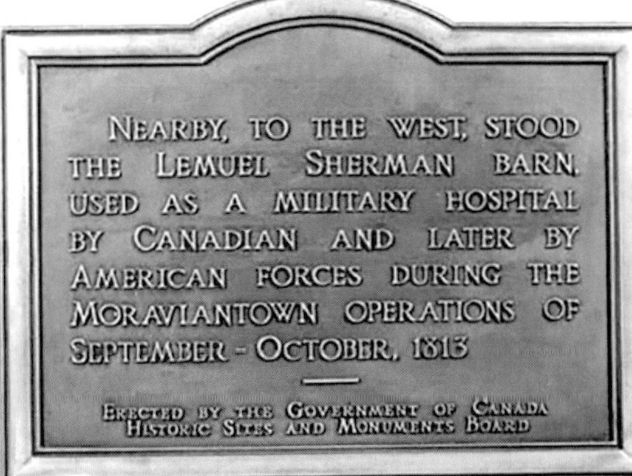

After the Battle of the Thames on October 5, 1813, both British and American wounded soldiers were housed in this barn on Lemuel Sherman's farm—some staying several months. The barn became a tourist attraction, as soldiers had carved their names or initials in some of the beams of the barn. Eventually, the barn was moved across the road on Highway 21, just south of the village of Thamesville where, unfortunately, it was consumed by fire in 1928.

Charles Helmer shows off the high water mark on his barn in Thamesville after the 1937 flood.

Cars are backed up on a flooded Highway 21 near Thamesville, 1937.

The Thames River reached its highest ever recorded level during the Flood of 1937. It also claimed more lives and damaged more property than any other flood, as these photos of Thamesville make clear. Many homes and businesses suffered catastrophic damage, at a time when the country was just beginning to recover from the Great Depression.

Thamesville's first "shopping mall" was located in the Spackman block on London Road between Ann and Lamilla streets, and featured a consortium of stores all under one roof. The upper floors held apartments for shopkeepers, as well as the Masonic Hall. Unfortunately, this shopping experience was shortlived; the building was consumed by fire on September 12, 1888.

This pre-1910 image of the main street of Thamesville shows the original town hall, before it burned. The building on the right, with the E.A. Evans Jeweller sign out front, was the Hubbel Block. Note the crooked telephone poles, wood sidewalks, abundant trees, unpaved street, and lack of motorized vehicles.

Mr. Jimmy Wealch of Thamesville purchased a brand new Model T in 1913 for $750. Thirty-one years later he was still driving the car, according to an article in the *Windsor Daily Star* on August 17, 1944. In all those years, he spent $40 on repairs, and in 1944, it was still giving him thirty-two miles to the gallon—a bonus in the days of wartime rationing. With a top speed of forty-five miles per hour, Jimmy put about 4,000 miles a year on the car.

The first town hall for Thamesville (then called Tecumseh) was constructed in 1875, a year after the settlement incorporated as a village. In 1890, this new, two-story brick building was constructed, but it burned on April 22, 1911. In the same year, construction began on a building that stands to this day.

The Martin Brickyard operated from the 1880s to 1930. Pictured here is Thomas Martin, who took over from his father in 1920, and his wife Mary Jane, in 1918.

Miss Sarah West taught in and around Thamesville for many years in the early twentieth century. She taught primary pupils in the Town Hall, and in the Presbyterian Sunday School hall in the 1920s, then moved to the public school on London Road. Miss West loved to travel and dress up. The museum at the Town Hall still has her mink stoles.

This postcard shows Victoria Street, which runs north and south in the town. Taken from the main intersection, looking south, the old post office is the first building on the left, while the third building on the right is the Tye Block, currently occupied by B's Hive.

This 1926 photograph of a newly paved London Road in Thamesville was taken from the traffic light, which is still the only one in town.

The hamlet of Wabash boasted an active and popular general store and post office, pictured here about 1904. The establishment was owned by Mr. and Mrs. Robert Kelley, who are seen proudly standing in front of their business.

Despite being tiny settlements, Turnerville, Tupperville, and Wabash all boasted brass bands. In 1914, the smartly dressed Cornet Band, pictured here, was asked to perform at the Camden-Dresden annual fall fair. The leader of this group was Alf Millben of Dresden, seen in the back row beside the snare drummer.

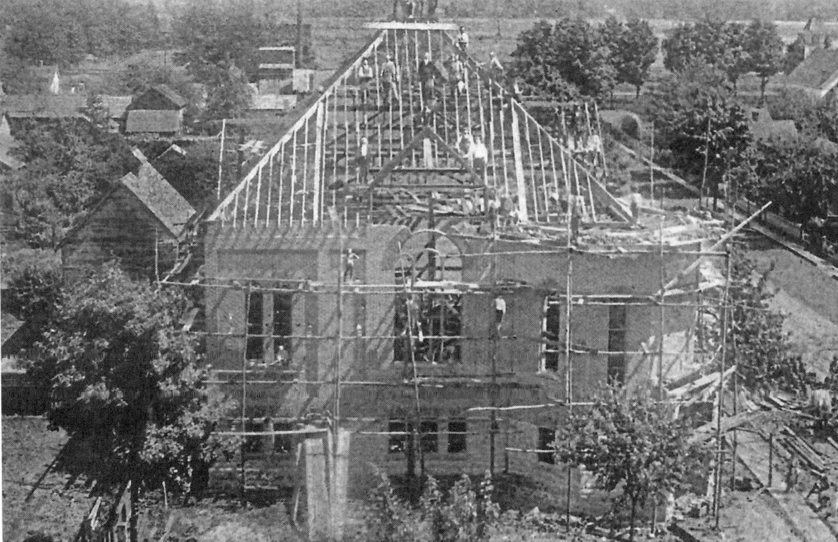

Built with Martin bricks, the Thamesville Methodist Church (in 1925, United Church) is seen here under construction in 1898.

The Tupperville Milling and Elevator Company, pictured here in 1902, was a co-operative venture that began in 1891. It was formed by attracting interested speculators who could buy in for ten dollars. It operated successfully until shareholders, short on money, started to cash in their investments, leaving the milling company insufficient funds to continue.

Anglican missionaries arrived on Walpole Island in 1842 to proselytize the First Nations communities there. They built this church on Walpole in the late nineteenth century, as well as a school.

Walpole Island Ferry, circa 1914.

Chief Peterwegeshick of Walpole Island is pictured here at age 106, with three generations of his family.

According to oral history, a First Nations village of about 200 people stood on the land later known as Kilbride's Farm, in the northern reaches of Dufferin Avenue in Wallaceburg. This tree, seen here circa 1950, was believed to be the result of an Indigenous practice of bending branches to mark trails. Unfortunately, this Dutch Elm succumbed to disease in the 1960s.

Pictured here circa 1902, is Wallaceburg's fire hall at the foot of Duncan Street, near the bridge. When the fire alarm bell rang in the station's belfry tower, volunteers rushed to the station while the firemen on duty quickly set to work lighting the boiler to fire up the steam engine. As an incentive, the first team to arrive at the station was awarded five dollars.

In 1923, the Wallaceburg Fire Department purchased its first motorized fire truck, consisting of a Bickle pump and tank on an International chassis. In 1929, they added a Reo chemical truck.

Bird's eye view of Wallaceburg, circa 1917. The Central Bridge spans the Sydenham River at right. A large load of lumber, ready to ship, is visible at the bottom. Beyond the river, three churches are partially visible: Our Lady of Help Catholic Church in the far distance with the tall steeple; Knox Presbyterian in the middle; and United Church at far left.

For over 150 years, the Lee family have played an important role in Wallaceburg, working in shipbuilding, machining, politics, and more. However, their name is most famously linked to the famed Lee-Enfield rifle; the original is the prized possession of the Wallaceburg and District Museum. Pictured here are Lee brothers James and John, who developed the rifle patent together.

For young Mabel Mann's birthday in 1905, her grandfather Sam took her and her friends on a ride around town. The wagon is seen in this picture pulling out of the barn at the corner of Lafontaine and Wellington streets, where Mann's Garage would be located for the next several decades. Sam (1845-1929) was the father of the legendary Wallaceburg historian Frank Mann (1896-1993) and grandfather to Alan Mann (1936-2009), who took on the mantle from his father.

The Mac-Craft Corporation was started by Eric MacDonald in 1938. He first built mahogany speed boats in a small shop at the foot of Hope Street in Wallaceburg. In 1939, the company moved to Nelson Street and continued pleasure boat construction until 1941, when the Second World War halted production and the company moved to Sarnia.

The Old River House at Wallaceburg was a pioneer hotel razed by fire in 1904.

By the 1880s, Wallaceburg was evolving from a rural lumbering village to an industrial community. In 1887, James Steinhoff teamed up with his entrepreneurial nephew, D.A. Gordon, to found the Steinhoff and Gordon Stave Mill, pictured here, situated on the east bank of the Sydenham River.

This historic photograph shows the birthplace of the famed Lee-Enfield Rifle on the banks of the Sydenham River in Wallaceburg. It was from the rear of this building that brothers James and John Lee proof tested the gun in 1879 by firing a bullet across the river.

According to local lore, a group of young Wallaceburg lads snuck into the belfry one night at the old public school on Lisgar Street and tied a long piece of binder twine to the bell. With an unravelled ball of twine in hand, they began ringing the bell from a distance. A gathering crowd, unable to spot the twine at night, determined that the old belfry was haunted. The next morning, a neighbour found the twine and unknowingly continued the prank by pulling the twine and ringing the bell—only to be discovered by the town watchman.

In 1907, Archie Hawken established the Hawken Milling Company, situated west of Murray Street, near the railroad tracks. Archie and his son Drader, who took over the firm in 1931, worked for the White Lily Company, producing the cleverly-named "U-Need-Me" pastry flour.

In 1905, D.A. Gordon, Herbert W. Burgess, and Herbert McDougall started another key industry: the Wallaceburg Brass and Iron Foundry. Here, a parade or trade-show float shows off products offered by the Brass Company in 1908.

After local sand deposits showed great potential in the creation of glass—and after a number of starts and stops—the Sydenham Glass Factory merged with the Diamond Glass Company to form the Dominion Glass Company in 1894. The factory, seen here circa 1908, would quickly become the backbone of the Wallaceburg community, soon to be known as the "Glasstown of Canada."

Travelling on dirt roads like James Street, pictured here looking east in the early 1900s, often produced ankle-deep mud in spring and large amounts of dust in the summer and fall. With these conditions, maintaining an average speed of three or four miles per hour on your horse was an accomplishment.

Wallaceburg Lawn Bowling Club, 1912. At the time, C.S. Miller was club president.

While Central Bridge was being repaired in the 1890s, the residents built a pontoon bridge (pictured above) by lashing three wooden scows together. In order to allow navigation, two spiles were secured a few yards east of the scows, permitting the middle scow to swing open. North Branch Bridge is also visible.

This beautiful photograph of Wallaceburg town centre after a snowfall in January 1949 was taken from Library Park by Bill Collins, the *Windsor Star*'s Wallaceburg photographer.

The paving of James Street, 1911. Visible in the background are Taylor's Garage and the Pearce Blacksmith Shop and Bakery.

Ruby "Jeanne" Gordon, daughter of local industrialist D.A. Gordon, debuted with the Metropolitan Opera Company on November 22, 1919. She returned to Kent County as an international star to give a benefit concert for the Public General Hospital on October 6, 1922.

In 1944, the H.J. Heinz Company established a processing plant. Pictured here circa 1945, the plant employed over a thousand workers during peak tomato season.

This fifty-home subdivision of Victory Housing was built in 1942-43 to accommodate factory workers employed in wartime industries. Most of the houses still stand today.

The first electric railway car connecting Wallaceburg with Chatham and Lake Erie arrived in 1905. However, the line was undermined by financial woes, unreliable service, local merchant complaints, and the rise of the motor car. It was discontinued in 1930.

Realizing the potential for growing sugar beets in the area, D.A. Gordon founded the Wallaceburg Sugar Company and built a factory in 1901. By 1909, the company merged with Kitchener's Ontario Sugar Company to form the Dominion Sugar Company. The increased need for farm labour resulted in a large influx of skilled workers coming from Belgium, Holland, and Czechoslovakia—many of whom remained in Kent County.

The two schooners shown in this early-1900s photograph being nudged into place by a large tug are the *Paisley* and the *Grampion*. The boats, which transported goods for a Dresden sugar company, were tugged backwards to Wallaceburg from Dresden as they were unable to move on their own up the narrow river.

Canadian figure skater Barbara Ann Scott opened the Wallaceburg Arena on December 12, 1949. Here, she plants a kiss on "Rink Mouse," the smallest Wallaceburg "Rink Rat."

Ditty Bags were cloth bags used by the Wallaceburg Red Cross ladies to send care packages to soldiers fighting the Second World War.

In 1944, the Central Bridge caught fire while under repair. The man walking across is druggist Frank Nightengale, rushing home to the south side. Both the bridge and Frank thankfully survived.

The Central Bridge, mid-swing, in 1912. By the 1940s, the bridge had been damaged by lake freighters that misjudged the structure's open position. The town even launched a lawsuit against one habitual culprit, the sand-sucker *John R. Emery*.

As a tribute to the war effort, the *HMCS Wallaceburg* was launched at Port Arthur, Ontario, in December 1942. A minesweeper during the war, she visited Wallaceburg in 1945, where the crew was feted and citizens were given free tours of the ship.

In June 1882, the water level of the Sydenham rose enough to sweep logs waiting to be rafted downstream into the river, leading to a log jam. As a result, crops were flooded and cattle drowned.

The war memorial, financed by Wallaceburg's own businessman and philanthropist Captain James Steinhoff, is shown in Library Park, where it was originally erected. Wallaceburg's Carnegie Library is visible behind it. The memorial was moved in 1975, when the library expanded.

In 1940, to boost wartime morale, a community-wide effort in Wallaceburg was made to beautify downtown buildings. Here, a number of painters are working on the old town hall on Duncan Street.

Wallaceburg's 700-seat Capitol Theatre opened in 1930, and was designed by C. Howard Crane—also responsible for Detroit's Fox Theatre. The theatre and its ornate Spanish decor lasted for forty years on James Street.

Silent movies, concerts, and talent shows in Wallaceburg found a home in the new Temple Theatre on the southwest corner of James and Creek streets, seen here circa 1920s.

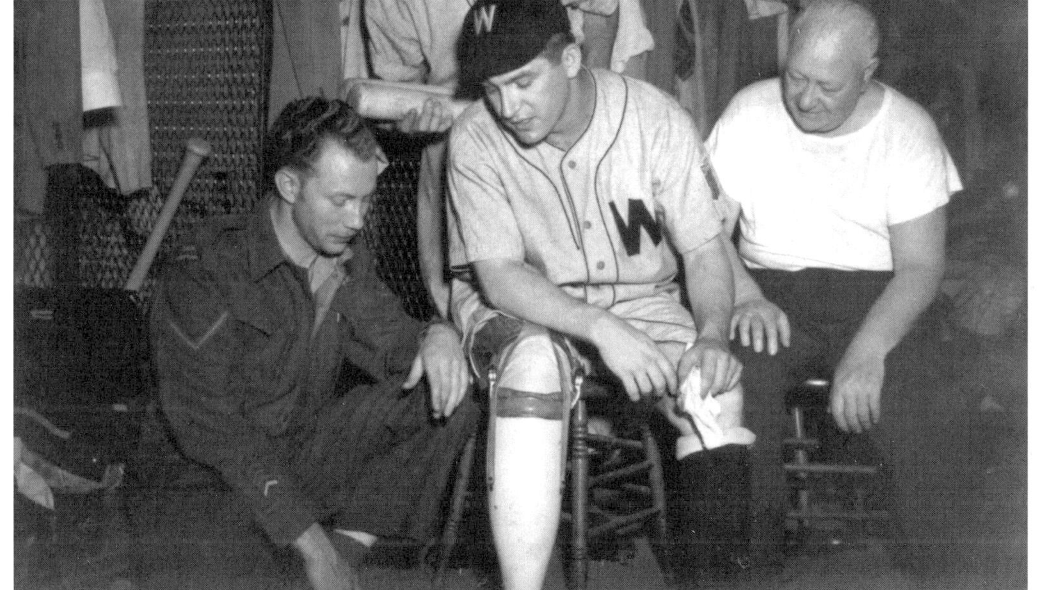

Don Errey, an amateur craftsman from Wallaceburg, was captured at Dieppe. Interned for the rest of the Second World War in Germany, he crafted artificial limbs for fellow prisoners of war—including for aspiring pitcher Bert Shepherd, who went on to pitch and later coach for the Washington Senators. Don (left) and Bert (seated) are seen here in the dressing room at Brigg's Stadium in Detroit in the summer of 1946.

After the demise of the Temple Theatre in 1939, a new theatre arose on the same spot, but with a more Hollywood persona. With its neon lights, the Alexander Theatre, seen here in the 1940s, was the talk of the town until it closed in 1954.

In 1944, to encourage the sale of Victory Bonds, the Amalgamated War Services branch suspended a mock Spitfire fighter plane, made in a Dominion Glass workshop, over James Street.

Selrite Department Store owner Morrison Irwin founded Mirwin Park in 1934 on the Snye River. The facility grew to include cabins, a hotel, several baseball fields, a large swimming pool, and according to some reports, a dance hall and a ferris wheel. In 1942, the Tip Sebe Hotel at Mirwin Park caught fire and burned, leading to the decline of the park. It was sold four years later.

Needing a publicity stunt, the Capitol Theatre in Wallaceburg had Scouts sell apples in the lobby in 1931. The idea was such a success that soon the fundraising "Apple Day" was held across Canada. Here, cub Henry Bushey sells 1947 Mayor Eric MacDonald an apple to officially launch sales.

International Harvester trucks from Chatham await shipment at the dock in Wallaceburg, August 1948.

With pomp and ceremony, the Lord Selkirk Bridge spanning the Sydenham River in Wallaceburg was opened to traffic on July 18, 1950. The photograph at right was taken from the south shore as the massive north link was lowered by hand from a near-vertical position to horizontal rest—a job that took two hours. When in operation, the electric motor performed the same task in about two minutes.

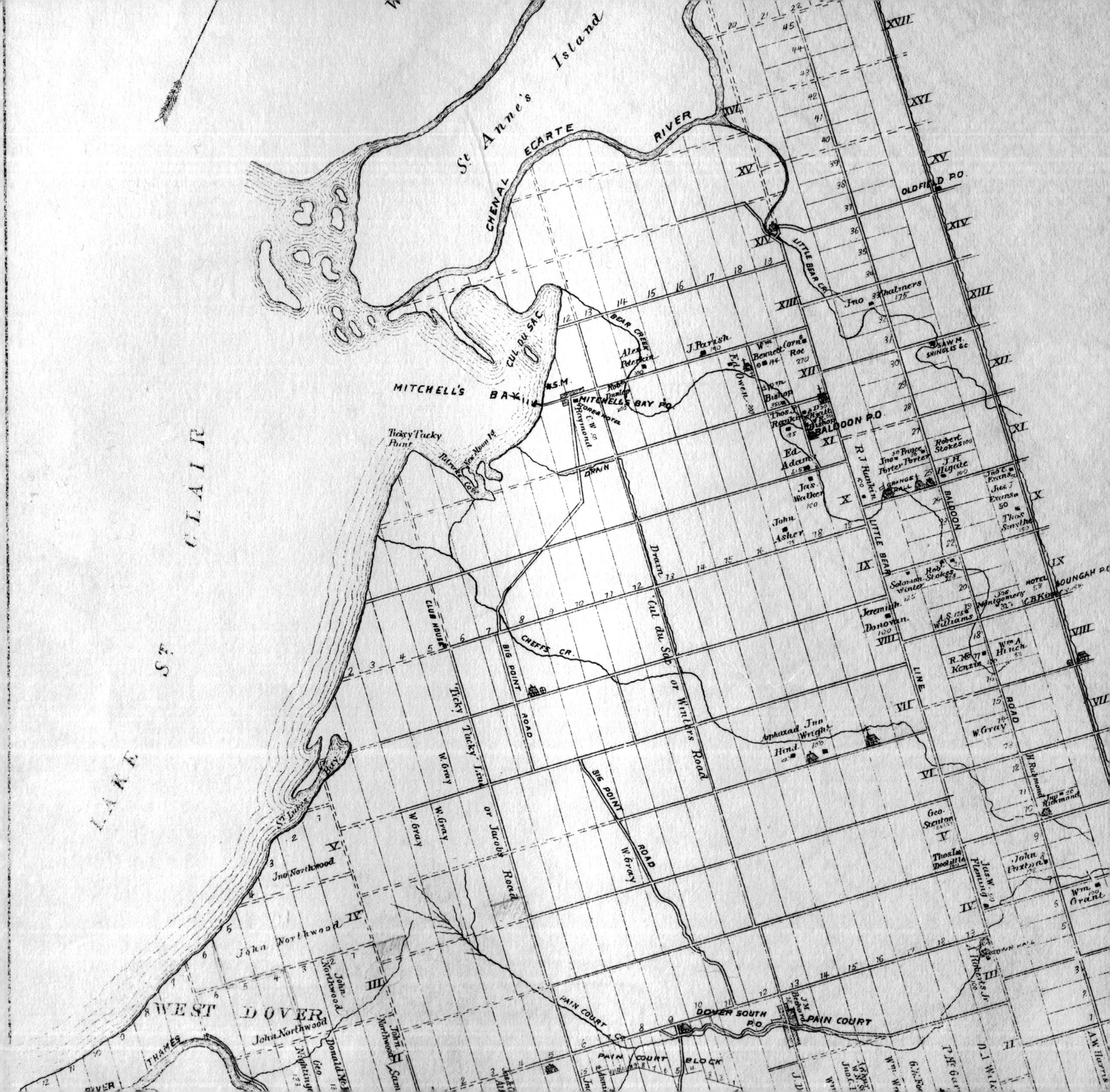

St. Anne's Island
CHENAL ECARTE RIVER
CUL DU SAC
MITCHELL'S BAY
MITCHELL'S BAY P.O.
LAKE ST. CLAIR
Ticky Tacky Point
BEAR CREEK
LITTLE BEAR CR.
OLDFIELD P.O.
BALDOON P.O.
SAW M. SHINGLES &C
GRANGE HALL
BALDOON ROAD
LITTLE BEAR LINE
DRAIN
Cul du Sac or Winters Road
CHEFFS CR.
CLUB HOUSE
BIG POINT ROAD
Ticky Tacky Line or Jacobs Road
HOTEL
WEST DOVER
THAMES RIVER
PAIN COURT
DOVER SOUTH P.O.
PAIN COURT BLOCK
TOWN HALL
J. Parish
Alex Peterkin
Wm Bishop
Ed. Adams
Jas. Walker
John Asher
R J Hankin
Robert Stokes
J.H. Higate
Jno Chalmers
Solomon Winter
Jeremiah Donovan
A.S. Williams
R. McKenzie
W. Gray
Jno Wright
Geo. Stenton
John Paxton
Wm Grant
Jno Northwood
John Northwood

CHAPTER TWO
Northwest Kent

When we divided old Kent County into sections, we included only one township, an admittedly large one, within our northwest boundaries. Technically, this area does not represent a quarter of the county, but the communities it contains played an important historical role.

Dover Township, then, occupies that part of Kent County which lies to the west of the Chatham/Dover townline, now known as Highway 40. The southern boundary is the Thames River, with Lake St. Clair comprising the western and also much of its northern boundary, the rest being taken up by the Chenal Ecarte (Snye). The land in Dover is noted for its fertility, even in a county that has some of the best farmland in Canada. However, much of the land along the Thames, and reaching northward along Lake St. Clair, was uninhabitable swampland until the drainage schemes of the later nineteenth century made this area usable and productive.

Perhaps this is why fewer small communities were established in Dover Township than in other parts of the county. Most of these settlements developed later, when better roads and the railroad eliminated the need to provide wayfaring places for travellers to rest.

One important early community in Dover was the Dolsen Settlement. Matthew Dolsen arrived with the first group of United Empire Loyalists, settling along the Thames as early as 1792. He soon developed a building complex that provided essential services for pioneers. That complex included a trading post, a blacksmith shop, a distillery, and a tavern. There was even a dock, where his ship—said to be the first ship on the Thames—was used for loading and unloading all the products used at the settlement and elsewhere.

The Dolsen Settlement became the unofficial capital of the Lower Thames. Every traveller who came to these parts, including Sir John Graves Simcoe in 1793, stayed at Dolsen's. The British army also camped here on the night of October 3, 1813, on their disastrous retreat up the Thames. For a time, it looked likely that the battle with the Americans would take place right here, rather than near the Moravian settlement of Fairfield.

Another noteworthy early settlement was founded by a man who left a big mark on Canadian history. Thomas Douglas, Lord Selkirk—whose more famous settlement was the Red River colony in Manitoba—also brought a number of Highlanders to Kent County, to the very northern reaches of Dover Township along the Chenal Ecarte (Snye). The Highlanders arrived in 1804, but by 1815 the settlement had been broken up, with some settlers staying on the original tract and others leaving to find their own way. The land was just too low; water not only spoiled crops on a regular basis, but it also made many of the settlers sick. Nevertheless, the Baldoon settlement, as it was called, wasn't a complete failure because it spawned new communities. Many of its settlers moved on to Bear Creek, a little inland, which would eventually become Wallaceburg.

Before we move on, a little backtracking is necessary. As mentioned in other places in this book, the earliest settlers "squatted" on land around the mouth of the Thames. That being said, possibly the earliest settler in Dover Township was a fascinating Oneida woman named Sally Ainse. Born in 1728 in present-day New York State, she later became an important fur trader, based at Fort Detroit and Fort Michilimackinac. In 1783, she purchased a parcel of land between the mouth of the Thames to the forks at later-day Chatham, on the north bank of the river, from the Ojibwa, and moved here to retire. Unfortunately, when the British arrived, she was cheated out of these lands, and ended up with only one lot on the Thames, Lot 10.

A few years after the first influx of early settlers, a group of French Canadians arrived in Dover Township. Families like the Paquettes, the Babys, and the Peltiers established the strong French Canadian complexion still maintained by the township. These settlers also claimed land on the Thames and later moved inland. Many of them settled along a creek that later was given the same name as the community they founded: Pain Court.

In time, other inland parts of Dover Township were settled, along Baldoon Road and the Bear Line. As discussed, the township was stymied in its progress by the wet conditions in much of its western and northern reaches. Development would have to wait until 1878, when Samuel Thomas Martin took a risk and bought 600 acres of Dover marsh for seventy-five dollars. Martin was a real estate developer, not a farmer, and he was determined to make the swampy land profitable. By 1880, he had invented the Martin "Scoop" Waterwheel. His neighbours scoffed at the idea of making something out of swampland, but Martin astounded his critics by leading a wave of innovators to develop variations of waterwheels and pumps. It took a few years, but eventually the Dover swamps were transformed into remarkably fertile farms.

Other innovations in farming—in particular motorized tractors and threshing machines, as well as developments in the marketing and selling of crops—eventually made the life of a Dover farmer much easier. Improved roads and communication also made for less isolation. Throughout all of the issues and world events, the land still provided for the people of Dover Township. Today, Dover Township—the northwest of old Kent County—remains one of the world's finest agricultural areas.

This cabin is believed to belong to Sally Ainse, possibly the earliest settler in Dover Township. An Oneida princess and successful fur trader, she amassed enough money to buy from the Ojibwe all the land from the mouth of the Thames to the Forks at the future site of Chatham, on the north bank, one lot deep. After the McKee purchase, the Land Board ignored Ainse's claims and she was denied all but one of her 200-acre lots.

Dolsen Settlement, as sketched by John Howison, 1820. The settlement's namesake was Matthew Dolsen, a United Empire Loyalist, who'd settled along the Thames as early as 1792. Dolsen's wife, Hannah, was the unofficial doctor of the area in the early days. When the Americans came knocking during the war of 1812, she faced them down alone, as Matthew had died a few weeks earlier.

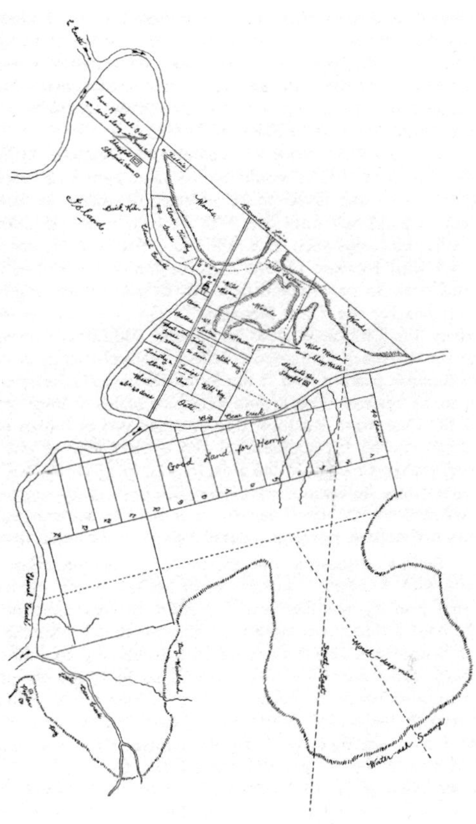

In 1792, Alfred Douglas, Lord Selkirk, launched a plan to resettle Highlanders, dispossessed by the Clearances, in Canada. In 1804, a group of Scottish refugees settled on land by the Chenal Ecarte (Snye River) in northern Dover Township. They called it Baldoon. Baldoon provided many hardships: lack of housing, swampy land, disease and isolation, plus raiding Americans during the War of 1812. By 1815, Lord Selkirk withdrew his support, and many settlers—now free to move—sought higher, dryer land in places like Wallaceburg.

The school pictured here is likely S.S. No. 4, built at the intersection of the 7th Concession and the Winter Line around 1900 and the last frame school house in Grande Pointe. In 1912, a new brick school was erected on Lot 9 of 8th Concession.

In 1882, Father Bauer, parish priest for Grande Pointe, was authorized to build a $6,000 church, named St. Philippe Apotre. This church lasted for almost seventy years, until it was dismantled in 1949. A new Gothic structure was erected a mile away, at the Winter Line.

Perhaps one of Upper Canada's earliest ghost tales, the Macdonald house (pictured here) in Baldoon, was believed haunted in the 1830s. The house sat on desirable land, and when the Macdonalds refused to sell, the poltergeist attacks increased. Broken windows, self-combusting fires, boomeranging rocks—all believed to be the work of a neighbouring old woman. After travelling some eighty-two miles to Long Point to consult a girl with "second sight," Mr. Macdonald shot a black goose he'd spotted on the property, in the wing. Shortly after, the old woman was seen with a broken arm and the haunting mysteriously stopped.

Joseph Cheff arrived in Grande Pointe in 1845 and started a critical industry: the sawmill. Seen here in 1930, after being sold to the Tetrault family, the mill operated until the 1940s.

This stop on the Chatham, Wallaceburg and Lake Erie (CW&LE) Electric Railway was named Electric in the early 1900s. In 1909, J.C. Kearns of Chicago started a general store in Electric that was soon joined by a post office. The Kearns Store survived the 1930 closure of the CW&LE, closing its doors in 1968.

French-Canadian settlers called this part of North Dover "la grande pointe," referring to the jagged land extending into Lake St. Clair. The settlement of Grande Pointe was formed in the 1880s. In 1882, it was granted a post office, even though the settlement was considered to be part of the "mission of Pain Court" by the Catholic Church until 1886. Pictured here are two early settler families: the Benoits (left) and the Labadies (right).

Mr. and Mrs. Calixt Benoit started a grocery business at 9th Concession and the Winter Line in 1915. Pictured here in 1930, the store's inventory included yard goods, hardware, drugs, shoes, horseshoes, and even Ford auto parts. The store also offered a delivery service, accepting eggs and butter in exchange for groceries.

In 1897, Francis Dubuque built the Halfway House on the 8th Concession halfway between Pain Court and Grande Pointe. A popular watering hole, the hotel was shuttered during Prohibition, only to be later re-opened as a pub by Fred Ouellette. The building burned in 1984.

The Martin Family started growing popping corn on their farm in 1934, starting with two acres. Prior to 1939, the Martins were the only growers of popcorn in Canada. Pictured here circa 1940, the farm had expanded to 1200 acres by 1946. The business was sold in 1978.

The first place of worship for the French-Canadian settlers to the Pain Court area was a small wooden chapel built in 1851-2. A second, larger church was built two years later, but it burned in 1874. Here, the congregation lays the cornerstone for the third church in 1911.

The third church in Pain Court, Imaculee Conception Church, was built at a cost $50,000. The pride of local parishioners, this ornate structure boasted a large nave, beautiful altar, and many windows. The parish manse is visible to the left of the church.

The burnt-out shell of Immaculee Conception Church, 1937. The Virgin Mary statue survived the fire and can be seen beneath the destroyed steeple.

The Primeau and Bourdeau General Store in Pain Court, early 1900s.

In 1910, the electric railroad (CW&LE) built a spur line extending from Chatham to Pain Court. Seen here in 1914, the line ran at the north end of town where Winter Line meets the Fourth Concession. This posed shot displays two automobiles, the railway tram, and the Dover Hotel. Despite this idyllic scene, the rail line inflated farm prices from $150 per acre to over $300.

This aerial shot shows the fourth church in Pain Court, circa 1953. The convent and the church presbytery are visible to the left, as well as Ecole St. Catharine elementary at right and the new secondary school in the distance.

In 1859, Pain Court's post office was named "Dover South," after the government refused the name "Immaculee Conception," calling it "too French" and "too Catholic." Rebuffed, settlers petitioned for "Pain Court," meaning "short of bread"—alluding to the harsh conditions faced by early settlers. By 1911, the Postmaster General had agreed.

In 1911, T.H. Taylor decided to expand his grain elevator business out to Pain Court, meaning local farmers could sell their grain closer to home rather than trekking to Chatham. The mill is pictured here circa 1950s.

The Central Hotel in Pain Court, circa 1909. At right, the bar inside the hotel is pictured a few years later.

The Pain Court Baseball Team, 1906. The boys are sitting outside the Dover Hotel, then owned by D.D. Gagner Sr. In the front row, from left, are: Willie Bayer, Andre Roy, Amede Bechard, D.D. Gagner Jr., Edward Bedard, and Louis Bechard. In the back row are: Alphonse Ouelette, Trefle Gagner, Felix Bourassa, and Herbert Bourdeau. Behind them is Napoleon Bourassa, coach and manager.

Students in a classroom at Ecole Chez Etienne in Pain Court, circa 1930.

The Primeau and Bourdeau General Store in Pain Court, early 1900s.

Bruce Foster Bradley (seen at far right) arrived in Dover Township in 1912 to manage 1655 acres of farmland at the mouth of Thames. Bruce established Fertile Meadows Farm, one of the most important farms in Kent County. Today, the company is Brad-Lea Meadows.

The main street of Dover Centre, 11th Concession, is shown here in the early 1900s. When the CW&LE arrived on Baldoon Road, the crossroad in this image, roads were still unpaved and terribly muddy. The story goes that in the 1880s, Mrs. Donald Angus would walk barefoot to Dover Centre Presbyterian Church, seen at left, carrying her shoes so they wouldn't be dirtied. The church seen here was constructed in 1913 after a frame church with a magnificent pipe organ burned earlier that year. Even in 1948, the congregation was still raising funds for a new organ.

Weeders on Fertile Meadow Farms in Dover Township, circa 1930s.

Marjory Sigler Bradley—seen here at centre, standing in the lake pasture—was essential to the success of Fertile Meadows Farm. Coming from an affluent family in Cleveland, Ohio, she married Bruce in 1916 and moved with him to the farm in Dover Township. Her money helped keep the farm solvent at times, and she participated fully in the business.

During the Second World War, the government sent Japanese-Canadian men to many work camps in Ontario. Pictured here is the internment camp at Dover Centre, where the men were required to do farm labour. The building was also used to house German POWs between 1943-46.

In 1897, the Women's Institute was founded in Stoney Creek, Ontario, and quickly spread across the province, including to Kent County. Here, members of a local chapter commemorate the organization's fiftieth anniversary. Each chapter met at least once a month, usually with a speaker or to learn a new skill. The organization was empowering for rural women, giving them a voice outside the home.

St. Luke's Bay, just south of Mitchell's Bay, on the eastern shore of Lake St. Clair, was a favourite (albeit less famous) spot for duck hunting and fishing. This local fisherman shows off his catch from St. Luke's Bay in 1947.

By the 1940s, Mitchell's Bay on Lake St. Clair in Dover Township was a popular fishing hole for visitors—including entertainers Roy Rogers and Dale Evans, pictured here with a local boy. The couple came every summer for some years to fish and relax away from the spotlight.

Mitchell's Bay has many small islands, which cottagers bought up in the early twentieth century. Here, lifetime resident, island caretaker, and commercial fisherman Bruce Macdonald is pictured on one of the islands in the 1940s.

For ice-fishing enthusiasts at Mitchell's Bay, Al Shain devised an ice-fishing charter craft, which skimmed over the frozen water on a motor-driven propeller.

Fertile Meadows Farm, 1913. The Thames River is at left, with Lake St. Clair in the distance. As signified by the geese, a wildlife refuge still exists at Bradley Farms. Swamps like this persist as well.

GREAT WESTERN RY
THAMESVILLE P.O.
NORTHWOOD P.O.
ARNOLD'S CR.
MORAVIANTOWN
INDIAN RESERVE
BOTANY P.O.
BRIDGEND
MC GREGORS CR.
HARWICH P.O.
TURIN P.O.
HARWICH CENTRE P.O.
HARWICH CROSSING
CENTRE LINE
COMMUNICATION RD
ERIE AND HURON RY
Gravel Road
HOWARD
WELDON P.O.
ORFOR
HARWICH
HIGHGATE P.O.
STA.
RIDGETOWN P.O.
Township Line Range
HOWARD ROAD
MIDDLE OR RIDGE ROAD
MUIR KIRK
RONDEAU P.O.
BLENHEIM
FAIRFIELD P.O.
WEST TROY
BUCKHORN P.O.
GUILDS P.O.
TALBOT ROAD
MORPETH P.O.
Con I
PALMYRA P.O.
RONDEAU HARBOUR P.O.
RAGLAN
SHREWSBURY
BISNETTS TRAMWAY & DOCK
MORPETH DOCK
WILSONS DOCK
DOCK
PORT CLEARVILLE
RONDEAU
PIER
POINT AUX PINS
LAKE ERIE

CHAPTER THREE
Southeast Kent

Southeast Kent consists of the section of the old county bounded on the north by the Thames River, on the south by Lake Erie, on the east by Aldborough Township in Elgin County, and on the west by Raleigh Township. Within its boundaries are the townships of Orford, Howard, and Harwich. Communities found here today include Blenheim, Ridgetown, Morpeth, Shrewsbury, Rondeau, Erieau, Erie Beach, Highgate, Duart, Muirkirk, and Palmyra. The Delaware First Nations reserve, also known as Moraviantown, is also included in this section's boundaries. Southeast Kent is also home to many ghost towns including Guilds, Troy, Eatonville, Clearville, Botany, Northwood, Turin, Rushton's Corners, Clachan, Howard Bridge, Harwich Centre, Antrim, New Scotland, Fargo, and Raglan. Needless to say, Southeast Kent has had the largest number of communities, past and present, develop within the otherwise rural sections of the region.

Like other areas of the Kent, the southeast was first settled by Europeans along the waterways. The banks of the Thames River saw settlers as early as the 1790s. Frederick Arnold and his sons were among the first, arriving in Howard township in 1796. He set up a grist mill along Arnold's Creek, not far from the Thames. The mill was essential for farmers needing their grain ground into flour. A nearby ford in the Thames acted as a crossing for settlers. In 1826, a bridge was spanned across, and the early settlement came to be known as Howard Bridge.

The Moravians and the Lenape people of the Delaware Nation had returned to the Thames after the War of 1812. They decided to settle across the river, in the northern reaches of Orford Township. The Moravians remained there until 1901. The Delaware Nation reserve remains today. The government induced them twice into giving up some of their land—which was then opened to European settlers. Many First Nations on the reserve contrived to farm, as they had before the war.

The shores of Lake Erie also saw early settlement. John Craford settled near the mouth of Patterson's Creek, just east of Pointe aux Pins (Rondeau) in 1809. The Ruddle family arrived about a mile down the shore at the mouth of Big Creek in 1815, where they began to develop the harbour there. At one point the hamlet named Antrim that grew around the harbour contained a store, a tavern, and a trading post, and the harbour bustled with both exports and imports. There was even a small shipbuilding concern. By the late 1840s, however, Antrim began to lose business to its rival further up Big Creek, along the Talbot Trail: Morpeth.

Many of these later settlements developed along the Talbot Trail. Colonel Thomas Talbot's colonization scheme, which began in Elgin County, had spread to the east and west.

Mahlon Burwell, Talbot's surveyor, had just begun to survey the road and lots immediately adjacent to it when the War of 1812 intervened. Burwell resumed his work in 1815, and by that time Talbot was inundated with requests for lots.

One of the first communities was set up at Clear Creek, just west of the county line. John Bury and his family were the first to come in 1816, followed a year later by David Baldwin. By 1825, Baldwin had established a tavern along Talbot Road, which became the centre of the Clearville community. He was followed, in 1832, by George Henry, who built the much-needed grist mill at the mouth of Clear Creek. The village developed along the creek between the lake and the Talbot Road.

The story of Morpeth's growth is typical of the area's settlements. Morpeth was located just west of a large gully that proved a mighty obstacle to local travellers and their wagons. Repairs were often necessary after a wagon had reached the other side of the gully, and Morpeth developed to meet those needs. By the mid-1830s, Morpeth was a thriving mercantile centre. In the 1860s, it was rivalled in Kent only by the county seat, Chatham.

The Talbot Road was considered to be one of the best roads in Upper Canada, but when it reached the Howard/Harwich townline, it broke down. At that point, travellers were forced to turn northwest, towards Troy on the ridge, and travel thence towards Chatham. This road was also in very poor condition. Chroniclers at the time, including Bishop Strachan, who came through in 1828, and Anna Jameson, who visited in 1837, all mention the terrible road conditions, no matter what the weather, as well as the lack of decent accommodations.

There were two reasons for this problem. The land along the lower ridge in Harwich was quite swampy, with Rondeau Bay quite close. In fact, an early settlement along the bay, called Shrewsbury, had been plotted by Simcoe's orders in the 1790s but no one had settled there because of the wet conditions. The other reason was because the land in Harwich had early been taken up by absentee owners, speculators who had no intentions of ever performing their settlement duties. In fact, there was such a lack of development that the area was known for many years as the Ten-Mile Bush.

However, eventually even that land was occupied. The land in Harwich had also been claimed by speculators who had no intention of performing their settlement duties. Colonel Little platted a village called Blenheim. For many years, Blenheim's growth was slow, but by the 1880s it was developing into what would become the most populous community in South Kent. Why? The railroad had come to town.

The railroad offered a faster and better means of transportation than the horse-drawn conveyances on the roads. When the Canada Southern Railway laid a line across the southeastern part of the county, the communities along the Talbot Road were too far north to benefit from the railway. The new line favoured communities along the ridge, places like Muirkirk, Highgate, and of course, Ridgetown.

Ridgetown was settled in the 1820s, but like Blenheim, its development was sluggish. The railroad brought new business and industry with it. Ridgetown overtook all other villages in southeast Kent, except Blenheim, and when the Detroit River and Lake Erie railroad also came to Ridgetown in the 1890s, the community's future development was secure.

The railroad, however, did not remain the most favoured form of transportation. Not long after the railroad arrived in the area, the automobile was invented. It took a while to develop the necessary infrastructure and for the cost of automobiles to come down, but the car eventually superseded the railroad. But by then it was modern times, another story for another time.

The Pardo Sawmill on John Street in Blenheim, 1896. The man behind the reins of the carriage is most likely the owner, Mr. T.L. Pardo.

Situated on the corner of Old Street (the Old Talbot Trail) and Highway 3, this gas station was a popular spot just outside of Blenheim in the 1930s. It sat across from what is today the Willow Run golf course, and was part of Whittington Camp, which offered rental cabins and gasoline for travellers. The pumps were Thayers Standard Gasoline ten-gallon pumps.

Here, Frank Ford drives a horse-drawn funeral coach in front of the family business: Ford and Sons Furniture and Undertaking. The building was constructed in 1877. Frank was the second of four generations of Fords to run this business in Blenheim.

In 1883, Blenheim became a station on the Erie and Huron Railway, which later became the Pere Marquette Railway. Seen here in 1903, the PMR added a lunch counter to the station soon after acquiring the building. By 1926, an average of fifteen Pere Marquette freight trains passed through Blenheim every day.

On May 19, 1790, Alexander McKee, a British Indian agent and representative of the Ottawa, Potawatomi, Ojibwa, and Wyandot nations, signed a treaty, giving title to much of what became Southwestern Ontario to the British Crown. The former fairgrounds in Blenheim mark the event with a cairn to the transaction, now known as the McKee Purchase.

Starting in the 1840s, William Pegg's one-horse cart went door to door, allowing Blenheim residents to fill their jugs from one large milk container. By the time this picture was taken in 1925, the Blenheim Dairy had been purchased by William and Lottie Neil and offered "pasteurized" products.

In this early photograph, Capuchan monks stand in front of their monastery called St. Francis in Blenheim. The parish church, St. Mary's, was located across and down Chatham Street. The monastery was recently demolished.

Blenheim's two-storey town hall, seen here circa 1950, was constructed at the corner of Talbot and George streets in 1896. The impressive structure had twin towers (one for fire lookout), and a concert hall—the "Opera House."

A spring smelt run is pictured here along Lake Erie in 1947. Smelting continued to be popular until recent years when, sadly, the smelt stocks diminished.

In the early 1900s, Blenheim's annual Agricultural Fair was held in what today is Blenheim Memorial Park. The event was designed to promote farming and agriculture, but also featured entertainment like balloonists, acrobats, early parachutists, and medical expos—plus an annual pigeon shoot.

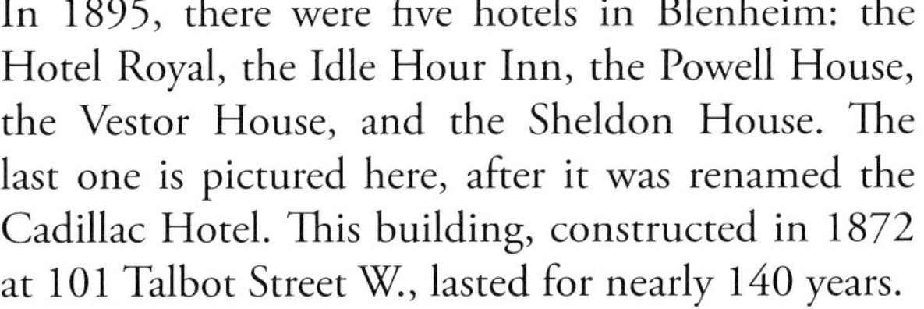

In 1895, there were five hotels in Blenheim: the Hotel Royal, the Idle Hour Inn, the Powell House, the Vestor House, and the Sheldon House. The last one is pictured here, after it was renamed the Cadillac Hotel. This building, constructed in 1872 at 101 Talbot Street W., lasted for nearly 140 years.

After the First World War, many young men who had served in the Royal Air Force still craved the adrenaline rush of flying, so they became "barnstormers," putting on exhibitions at local fairs and special performances. One such daring display happened in Blenheim, when a former ace pilot named Stewart Buzzard, who built his own plane, convinced the town to allow him to use Talbot Street (seen here) as a runway!

Reginald Delmer Snobelen was the first farmer in Kent County to own a gasoline-powered tractor. It was a Case 4 cylinder machine, with a four cylinder engine that he operated on his Bisnett Road farm. Snobelen gained national attention when the *Toronto Weekly Sun* featured him and his tractor on October 25, 1916.

Blenheim boasted its own "Flat Iron Building," as uniquely shaped as its more famous counterparts in New York and Toronto. Here, it is seen in its original iteration, as the J.W. Gibson Jewellery Store from the 1880s. The building still stands at the corner of Talbot Street and Catherine Street.

T.B. Shillington is jauntily perched on the open door of his delivery wagon for his line of ready-made men's clothing. Shillington also sold women's and children's fashions, plus yarn and patterns. This early photograph—likely an advertisement—was taken at the intersection of Talbot and Chatham streets, in front of the Powell House Hotel in Blenheim.

This 1908 dog-cart race took place on Talbot Street—that's Mott's Idle Inn in the background. The competitors include Doug Best, Archie McCormick, an unidentified boy, Babe Farnsworth, Wes Pickering, and Rule McKenzie.

Talbot Street in Blenheim, on the north side between George and Chatham streets, circa 1950. From left to right are Needhams, a furniture store and funeral parlour; Leighton & Glen Meat; Bert Brown groceries; Sim's Coffee Shop; the Temple Theatre, which opened in 1922 to screen silent films; and Rigby Motor Sales.

This 1918 bird's eye view of Blenheim's oldest residential area shows Ellen Street, with the Trinity Anglican Church at the centre of the photograph. Beyond the church is McGregor Street, with its impressive row of homes. Highway 98 is visible in the distance.

This stately brick home, pictured here in 1913, on the southwest corner of McGregor and George streets, was built in the 1880s for Dr. James Samson, the son of the Harwich Township pioneer, Mungo Samson. In time, the house was bought by Dr. C.B. Langford, and later still, by Dr. John Graham.

In the 1920s, James "Jimmy" Gordon started his own grocery store at 48 Talbot Street in Blenheim. He dedicated the next fifty-one years to growing the business, and in time, founded the chain of Gordon's Supermarkets that spread throughout Southwestern Ontario.

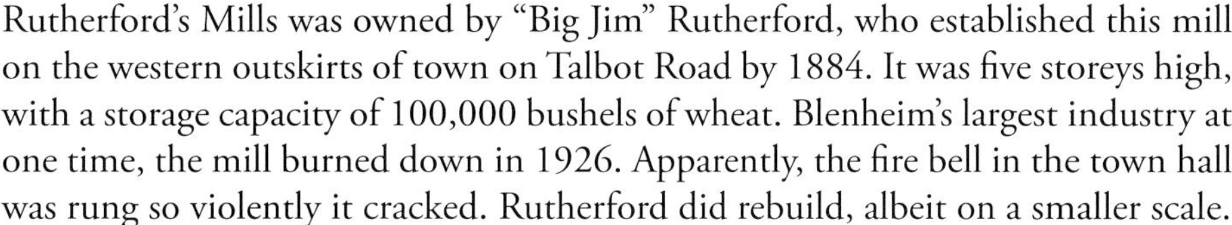
Rutherford's Mills was owned by "Big Jim" Rutherford, who established this mill on the western outskirts of town on Talbot Road by 1884. It was five storeys high, with a storage capacity of 100,000 bushels of wheat. Blenheim's largest industry at one time, the mill burned down in 1926. Apparently, the fire bell in the town hall was rung so violently it cracked. Rutherford did rebuild, albeit on a smaller scale.

Richard Porter, a barber from England, settled in Ridgetown in 1854. He built the block pictured here at 1 Main Street in 1878. It was the community's first three-storey building, featuring stores on the main floor, living quarters on the second, and an opera hall seating over a thousand on the top floor. Later purchased by John McKinlay, it was renamed the McKinlay Block, which it is still called today.

Talbot Street, Blenheim, 1930s.

The Canada Southern Railroad was supposed to run through Morpeth, along Lake Erie. However, in 1872, the plans were altered, and tracks were built a few miles north of the very small hamlet of Ridgetown, springboarding the community's expansion.

The Ridgetown Municipal Building, constructed in 1901, stood at 11 Erie Street South. It was a community centre in every sense until it was torn down in 1967.

The Arlington Hotel, at 30 Main Street W., was built in 1883 by the banker John Whyte. Over the years, the Arlington has survived a small pox quarantine, the great fire in 1899, and the local ban on alcohol in the early 1900s.

The Ridgetown water tower was erected in 1912 on the south side of William Street (now Ebenezer) on a parcel of land overlooking a long forgotten pond called Town Pond. In later years this site became Stennett Park.

Main Street, Ridgetown, circa 1903. At right, Jake Goldberg's business is visible, its marquis advertising that he is the "largest dealer in East Kent in old iron, rags, rubber, copper, brass, bear-hides, horse-hides, sheep-skins and raw furs." Just west of Goldberg's is William Baker's blacksmith shop, where he also built buggies in the "Victoria Carriage Works." Further down the street, the balcony of the Arlington Hotel is visible.

In 1904, the Ridgetown Bowling Association was formed, and it was not long afterwards that the greens on the corner of Ebenezer and Erie Streets were acquired for play. Shown here is most likely a Victoria Day or Dominion Day tournament.

High-school classes in Ridgetown originally began in 1883, with two rooms in the public school on Jane Street. One year later, this school was built at 8 Harold Street, after the owner, E.D. Mitton, offered a free plot of land. In 1886, the school attained collegiate status.

The first school to serve Ridgetown was on the Levi Cornwall farm, and in 1828 it had thirteen students—on a good day. After the community outgrew this and two other schoolhouses, the eight-room, two-storey building seen here circa 1900 was built on Jane Street in 1882.

On March 7, 1922, the government of Ontario purchased land from J.D. Brien in Howard Township, near Ridgetown, to establish the Western Ontario Experimental Farm. W. R. Reek, a known agriculturalist, was appointed as director. The house pictured here, circa 1930, was his residence.

W.R. Reek, the first director of the Western Ontario Experimental Farm, ran an educational program there from 1936-38. From this photograph of the Experimental Farm, it is clear that a great deal of pride went into its care.Today, the farm is part of the University of Guelph, Ridgetown Campus.

In 1879, the members of Ridgetown's Mount Zion Presbyterian hired renowned Detroit architect, W.G. Malcolmson, to build their new church. They directed him to build a steeple at least ten feet higher than the nearby Methodist steeple. Ironically, this same high steeple was blown down by a wind storm in 1906 and never replaced.

Most historians regard the building at 56 Main Street W. to be the oldest surviving building in Ridgetown. Built in 1855, newspaper ads reveal that by 1858, Dr. Jacob Smith—a physician, coroner, and dealer in patent medicines, groceries, oils, varnishes, and sundries—lived here. In later years, the building would play host to a Chinese laundry, a dry-cleaning shop, a real estate office, and a dental office.

Situated on Kent County Road 19 in Howard Township, on the western outskirts of Ridgetown, this house had been the focus of many a photographer and artist since it was abandoned in the 1930s. The house was originally constructed as a home for hired hands on the Scane farm, and it also had its own barn.

Master builder John Cooper built this house at 115 Main Street West for James McKinlay in 1881. McKinlay's wife, Jean Tallach, titled this house to her daughter, also named Jean, in her will. Miss Tallach worked for Henry Ford for many years as a buyer for his collection of artifacts at his Greenfield Museum and Village in Dearborn. This home was her summer residence.

When George Poag arrived in Ridgetown in 1892, he quickly set up his concrete construction business with his signature concrete blocks and bricks. These 'Poag Stones,' as they were called, were used to build the Poag home, seen here, at 95 Main Street East.

Tradition says that Morpeth was founded because of its location just west of this deep gully along the Talbot Road. Before the bridge was put in place, travellers needed a place to rest, after they managed to descend the cliff and cross the creek.

Morpeth's fate changed when the Canada Southern Railway abandoned plans to build a rail line along the shore of Lake Erie. In this shot of downtown from 1910, there are still several buildings on the main road, but new construction tailed off as Morpeth headed into decline.

Morpeth in its heyday, the 1860-70s. At the time, the town had four general stores, three hotels, one carriage factory, one cooperage, three blacksmiths, one carding and fulling mill, a foundry, a town hall, a lodge, and two churches. Its prime location on Talbot Road and Lake Erie helped make Morpeth the second largest community in Kent County in the 1860s.

The first town hall in Morpeth was built in the very early days of the community in the 1820s. Before the 1850s, the building truly was a township hall, but in 1855, Howard Township moved its capital to Ridgetown. Eventually, a new community hall was constructed on the northeast corner of Talbot Road and Main Street, where it stood until it burned down in 1983.

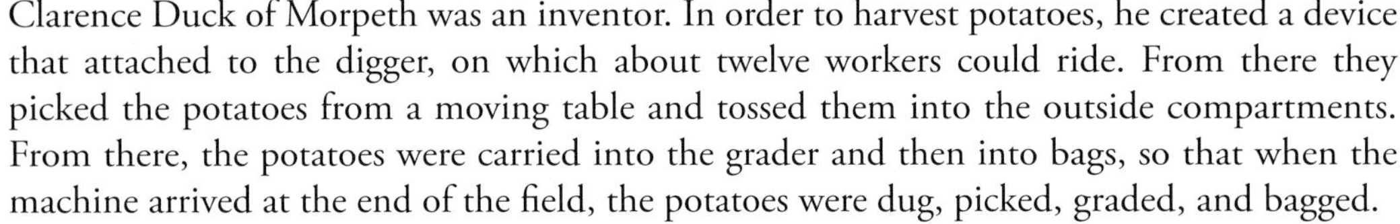

Clarence Duck of Morpeth was an inventor. In order to harvest potatoes, he created a device that attached to the digger, on which about twelve workers could ride. From there they picked the potatoes from a moving table and tossed them into the outside compartments. From there, the potatoes were carried into the grader and then into bags, so that when the machine arrived at the end of the field, the potatoes were dug, picked, graded, and bagged.

In 1861, the Canadian poet Archibald Lampman was born in the Anglican rectory in Morpeth. His father was pastor of Holy Trinity Church. The Lampman family moved when young Archibald was only six, but Morpeth claims him—one of the best Confederation poets in Canada—as their own. A federal memorial cairn was erected on the Trinity church grounds in 1930 in his honour.

In the 1850s, Shrewsbury became a haven for escaped slaves from the United States. One of them, Addison Smith, seen here with two of his daughters, told his story to a newspaper at age ninety-nine. Fleeing Tennessee, he eventually settled in Shrewsbury, where, with his third wife, he raised twenty-one children. He told the reporter that he wanted to live to be 110. In the 1908 Federal Election, he became the oldest person in Canada to cast a vote, at age 111.

In 1897, Rondeau's first official Park store was constructed south of the original dance pavilion. William Neil took over the Trading Post, as it was then called, in 1942, about the time this photograph was taken.

Charlie Grant established the Bayview Inn and Market, just outside Rondeau Park, in 1918.

Isaac Gardiner was appointed the first Superintendent of Rondeau Park in 1894, the year the park was established. His mandate was to attract visitors to the Park by offering various activities for campers and day visitors.

One of Superintendent Gardiner's first innovations was the introduction of deer to the park, which had none at the time. The first "guest" was a pet deer named Jerry, who had been raised from a fawn by a jail keeper in Sandwich (Windsor).

Tom was a bull moose also brought to Rondeau Park to attract visitors. With great living conditions and few predators, Tom grew to immense size. One day, perturbed by duck hunters shooting off their guns, he chased several of them into a cottage. Called to the scene, Superintendent Gardiner corralled the big moose, allowing the hunters to escape.

The second Rondeau Dance Pavilion opened in 1939, featuring a dining hall, lunch counter, and a wide, raised promenade circling the dance floor. Lee Simpson and Archie McDiarmid, the first concessionaires, oversaw the first dance on June 1, 1939, when more than 5000 people showed up to do some "Jitney Dancing." Unfortunately, this pavilion burned in 1973.

Although modern sensibilities may cringe at the thought of renting a bathing suit, this was common practice in the early 1900s. This photo from the 1930s shows a store at the end of the dock at Rondeau that rented suits.

Isaac Gardiner was not only Superintendent of Rondeau Park, he also created the Gardiner Family Band. Anxious to increase visitors to the Park, he successfully petitioned the government in 1895 to build a dance pavilion overlooking Rondeau Bay, seen here circa 1920.

In the 1890s, the Erie and Huron Railway, in conjunction with the Lake Erie and Detroit River Railway, ran a rail line into Erieau and began loading coal for delivery throughout Western Ontario. The coal was brought in to Erieau aboard coal boats, including the *Marquette & Bessemer No. 1,* seen here above, and the *Alexander Leslie*.

The Erie and Huron Railway built a line across the marshes east of Shrewsbury and onto the peninsula called Erieau. The line branched, with one line serving the coal hoists and the other transporting tourists. Note the Bungalow Hotel in the right foreground of this picture.

When you got off the train in Erieau, you were right on the doorstep of the Bungalow Hotel, which featured 100 guest rooms and ladies' and gents' porches. It opened in the 1890s and burned down in 1912. The Bungalow was never rebuilt.

The first recorded commercial fisherman in Erieau was Jack Julian in the 1850s. Within sixty years, commercial fishing would become a viable industry in town, providing many people with a good living. Goodison Brothers was one of the biggest fishing companies at Erieau, and in 1943, they began to also build ships here. These 1940s images show the extent of the fishing industry in Erieau.

Another popular resort at Erieau in the early 1900s was the Lakeview. Built by Charles Mallory, the resort became a social centre for the village. The building still stands and is occupied by the Bayside Brewing Co.

Shortly after the lighthouse keeper's house was moved in 1946, Erieau's lighthouse—situated at the end of the east pier—was torn down, as seen here.

In the 1890s, ferry service to and from Cleveland began from the pier at Erieau. As this scene from 1906 shows, it was a popular feature for many years.

The Huron and Erie Railway benefited from the influx of passengers as Erieau developed into a thriving summer resort. In response, the Chatham, Wallaceburg and Lake Erie Railway built this large pavilion right beside their railway stop in Erie Beach.

In 1946, the lighthouse keeper's home in Erieau was deemed unnecessary. Rather than tear it down, it was sold to Jim Goodhue and moved across Rondeau Bay where it stands today. A dry dock from Port Stanley was enlisted for the job, the house was pulled from its foundation and onto skids. This photo is from the collection of Verne Burke, whose father was the lighthouse keeper.

During the Second World War, Erieau held a record that was unbeatable in Canada. Every eligible man in the village was in service, plus four women—making sixty-nine persons enlisted out of a population of 235. Three volunteers lost their lives overseas, while many of those who returned gathered for this photograph after the war.

When John Reycraft purchased Crown land just east of present-day Highgate in 1857, he had no idea what the soil was hiding. It was not until 1886, when Reycraft was digging a ditch through the swale with Isaac Moorhouse and John Gosnell, that he discovered a "few bones of some extinct monster": a Mastodon tusk.

This collage of pictures, circa 1886, shows various people in the Highgate community with the unearthed Mastodon tusk, part of the discovery of "bones that kept coming and coming." The one tusk was measured and found to be nine feet, six inches long, and had been broken into three pieces. The other tusk was never found.

Newspapers from across Canada and the United States ran feature stories of the Highgate Mastodon discovery, heralding it as "one of the largest Mastodon skeletons ever found, not only in North America, but the entire world!" Reports claimed that there were enough bones to fill two wagons. This photograph from 1886 shows only part of the bones found, including four or five rib bones, a forty-seven-inch thigh bone, and a row of teeth seven inches across.

The Mastodon bones were lost for a time, but when they resurfaced they were sold to the University of North Dakota for $100 before Highgate could sue for possession. The bones remained in storage until 1991, when they were re-assembled at the North Dakota Heritage Centre.

After the pavilion at Erie Beach fell into disrepair and was torn down, a new generation of holidaymakers pitched their tents on the same site—a sign that camping had taken over as the new style of recreation.

This 1916 photo shows the original altar of the Highgate Methodist Church before fire destroyed it one year later. It was designed by the church's pastor, Rev. T.T. George. He was influenced by T.J. Rutley's Richardsonian-Romanesque design of First Presbyterian Church in Chatham.

The Gosnell family were early settlers in the Highgate region and their name survives there to this day. This photograph, taken around the turn of the century, shows the William James Gosnell family outside their well-kept early frame home.

Downtown Duart, circa 1905. A few horse-drawn sleighs make their way near the corner of St. Andrew's Road and the Middle Road. Bob Currie's post office and museum is visible at far right. Currie collected everything: arrowheads, stuffed birds, pistols, old tools, stamps, rare coins, and, he claimed, even a treasured meteorite.

Buck and Gert's Garage and Store in Duart featured a convenient sitting area right out front. Seen here circa 1934, the store became known as the place for car repairs and local gossip.

Dr. Duncan McPhail, seen here in the early 1920s, came to Highgate in 1887 to practise medicine, following a stint at Trinity College Medical School in Toronto. He also served as a member of county council and village council, the county coroner, a school trustee, doctor for Moraviantown, a member of three fraternity lodges, and a high-ranking Mason. He died after a shocking heart attack in December 1928.

As one longtime resident put it, "Highgate doesn't have a lot of fires, but when they do, they are spectacular." As seen in these *Chatham Daily News* photographs from January 1947, the three-storey feed mill in Highgate was hit by lightning and burned down. For many years, the mill housed the Canadian Cereal and Milling Company. The fire was so intense that debris from the mill fell across the Chesapeake and Ohio railroad tracks, blocking trains.

Tobacco farmer John Smith uses a horse-drawn plough on his farm in Muirkirk in 1949.

William Ker Muir was the president of the Canada Southern Railroad. As a tribute to this railway pioneer, local man John Carruth Campbell successfully lobbied to change the railway station from Duart to Muirkirk. Campbell argued that it was the coming of the CSR that gave the village its own personality and allowed it to grow. The westbound 45 is seen here heading into the Muikirk station, circa 1930s.

In 1872, the Canada Southern Railway was constructed in Muikirk, later to be taken over by the Michigan Central Railway. Mr. William Jones, pictured here circa 1900, was a regular driver who would meet the train with his stagecoach and take passengers, packages, and the mail bags to Duart.

This 1923 image shows a grain warehouse and mill crowded around the narrow Michigan Central station in Muirkirk. This wasn't the only railway to run through the community. In 1901, the Lake Erie and Detroit River Railway, later the Chesapeake and Ohio Railway, also came to town.

Horace Walker and Eastgate Humphrey are pictured here in 1909 at the Palmyra Sawmill, which stood just west of the Palmyra schoolhouse. As seen here, the yard around the mill would fill with logs during the winter and commence operations in the spring. One of their best customers was the Bates Fishery near Rondeau Park.

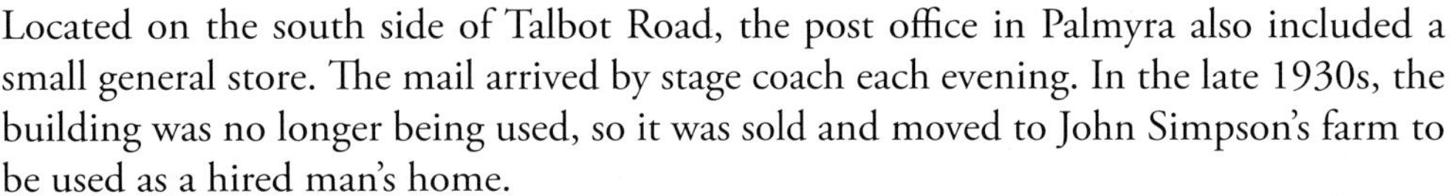

Located on the south side of Talbot Road, the post office in Palmyra also included a small general store. The mail arrived by stage coach each evening. In the late 1930s, the building was no longer being used, so it was sold and moved to John Simpson's farm to be used as a hired man's home.

Robert Barr (1849-1912) emigrated to Canada with his parents at age four, settling on a farm near Muirkirk. He attended the village school and went on to become a well-known author. In fact, his most famous creation, the detective Eugene Valmont, is often touted as the model for Agatha Christie's famous Hercule Poirot character. He is pictured here, at left, with Sir Arthur Conan Doyle in 1894.

The Palmyra Fishery was reportedly started in 1896 by a Mr. Swartz. Matthew Drivers & Sons, along with James Gray, operated the fishery for the next two decades. They transported the fish by army truck to Muirkirk and Ridgetown and then loaded the catch on train cars to be shipped to markets. The fishing shack, seen here in the early 1900s, was used from 1896-1956.

This 1910 picture shows a typical fishing scow used for driving net stakes into the lake bottom.

One of Kent County's first settlers was Frederick Arnold and his four grown sons, all United Empire Loyalists. They arrived in Howard Township in 1796, and soon after established the grist mill seen in this painting by an unknown artist. Also visible is the ford in the Thames which made for an ideal crossing point for travellers moving along the river in either direction. Howard Bridge, the first bridge across the Thames in Kent County, was built there in 1826.

New Scotland was a small community located along the Howard/Harwich townline, a few miles from Morpeth. New Scotland spawned a literary family of which Archie McKishnie was the novelist. His novel, *Gaff Linkum: A Tale of Talbotville*, is actually set in Morpeth, which he describes as "sitting on the crest of a great sloping hill, small but picturesque with its old fashioned houses and wide, old-fashioned streets surrounded by tracts of fertile land, much of it still wild and timpered."

In the 1860s, Johnson Soper purchased several hundred acres of bush and swamp along the north shore of Rondeau Bay and transformed it into productive farmland. Even the bricks that built his massive Victorian farmhouse were made from clay procured from the farm. James Clendenning (1847-1933) purchased the farm from the Sopers in 1904, and it remains in their family to this day.

The McKishnie family of New Scotland, Ontario, had more than one literary offspring. At age sixteen, Jean McKishnie Blewett wrote an award-winning poem entitled "Spring," launching a career as one of the most respected poets of her time. Also a noted journalist in Toronto, Jean even had a community in Saskatchewan named after her.

The United Church in New Scotland was first named after Rev. Dr. Albert Carmen, Superintendent of the Methodist Church. The settlement itself was at times called "the Reynolds Settlement" after a pioneer family or even "Carmen" after the church. Finally, when a post office came to town, the name "New Scotland," was adopted.

This photograph was taken along Lakeshore Road (today, Rose Beach Line), just west of Terrace Beach by L. Passmore of Ridgetown. The view looks west towards Rondeau Park.

Eatonville Hotel was built by J.A. “Pop” Eaton in 1926 for travelers making their way along Highway 3. Plagued by alcohol bans and the Depression, Eaton sold to Howard Pyne in 1936, who renamed the spot the Park Hotel (seen here). During the Second World War, the site became a federal internment camp for fifty-five Japanese-Canadian citizens. It still stands today.

A group of Scottish immigrants who settled on land near Lake Erie in the 1850s couldn’t decide where to construct a school. According to local legend, the school’s location would change from Sinclair Lane to Rondeau Bay Estates Line in the middle of the night. This stand-off was finally resolved when a site halfway between the two, on the Townline, was donated by William Reynolds in 1887, and a new brick school was built.

During the War of 1812, a British ship being pursued by the Americans reportedly threw barrels of gold overboard near Terrace Beach. While there are a few reports of single coins having washed up on the beach near the Morpeth Dock, no substantial coinage has ever been found.

At one time there were at least four fisheries operating in the Morpeth area. This is Peter Barker's fishery, circa 1909, with the Frank Rose fishery to the east. A bit further west was Coll's Fishery at Antrim and still further west was the locally famous Bates Fishery.

It did not take long for summer visitors to realize that cool summer breezes and beautiful views could be obtained by building summer homes on the cliff over Lake Erie. As early as the 1890s, summer homes of varying sizes, many of which still stand today, began to appear on the cliffs. Notice the expansive beach area that once existed at the foot of these cliffs.

W. DOVER
EAS
CHAT
DOVER SO P.O.
PAIN COURT
PAIN COURT BLOCK
BAPTISTE CR STA
BAPTISTE CR
JEANETTE CR
L.T.HO.
TILBURY STA
HENDERSON P.O.
EDGEWORTH P.O.
FLETCHER P.O.
CANADA
SOUTHERN
RY
NORTH BUXTON P.O.
CHARING CROSS P.O.
Gravel Ro
ERIE AND
THE DRAKE ROAD
CENTRE ROAD
BUXTON P.O.
TILBURY
EAST
RALEIGH
BACK LINE
VALETTA P.O.
TILBURY EAST P.O.
MIDDLE ROAD
BACK LINE
MERLIN P.O.
OUVRY P.O.
DEALTOWN P.O.
TALBOT ROAD
Gore
Eastern Division
Western Division
ROMNEY
ROMNEY P.O.
COATSWORTH'S ROCK

CHAPTER FOUR
Southwest Kent

Southwest Kent is bounded on the east by Harwich Township, on the south by Lake Erie, on the west by Mersea and Tilbury West townships in Essex County, and on the north by the Thames River. It includes the townships of Raleigh, Romney, and Tilbury East. Talbot Road ran through this section of the county as well.

This quadrant of Kent County attracted both the earliest European settlers to the area, and the last. It was here in the 1780s, before there was even an Upper Canada, that French Canadians from the Detroit River region started to settle along the lowest reaches of the Thames River, an area they called La Tranche. Names like Reaume, Lacroix, and Jacobs—familiar names even today—were recorded as owning land in what would become Tilbury East. Many of these deeds were sold to settlers by the Ojibwe. However, the British colonial government became concerned that this type of piecemeal land purchasing would become widespread. In response, they sent Department of Indian Affairs agent Alexander McKee to negotiate with the Ojibwe and other Indigenous groups. McKee's Purchase, resulting in the sale of a wide swath of what is today Southwestern Ontario, was completed in May 1790.

Other settlers soon arrived. Men like John Van Dolzen and his sons, Thomas McCrae and his family, and also the Peck, Drake, Parsons, and Toll families soon found land along the river in Raleigh Township. By 1796, a large community of families had settled there. It was these families who bore the brunt of the American invasion in 1813—but they also were the first to develop Kent as an agricultural area.

In Tilbury East Township, early settlers were dismayed in about 1830 when the water level of the Thames began to rise, leaving them with completely submerged farms. Famed naval novelist Captain Frederick Marryatt, R.N., who toured the area, said this in 1838: "These Canadians have not removed [...] their basements being under water, they occupy the first floors [. . .] As they cannot cultivate their land, they fish and shoot." Eventually, though, these French families did abandon their farms.

In the meantime, along the shore of Lake Erie, Colonel Talbot was continuing his westward push. As in southeast Kent, settlement slowly began along the Talbot Road in Raleigh, Tilbury East, and Romney townships in the wake of the War of 1812. In this area, the lake was largely inaccessible, separated from the land by large cliffs. Nevertheless, from 1817 to 1820, people like James Little, Samuel Pardo, and the Shepleys in Raleigh; Peter Simpson and Thomas Askew in Tilbury East; and Robert Coatsworth and Peter and Joseph Heatherington in Romney became the pioneers of later settlements in southwest Kent.

Middle Road was carved out of the landscape, further inland, between the 1820s in Raleigh and the years after the

1838 Upper Canada Rebellion in Tilbury East. The interior of the townships was heavily wooded, and settlers often lost their way in the wilderness. Despite this drawback, many communities had sprouted up along the thoroughfare by the middle of the century, including Cook's Corners (later Charing Cross), Merlin, Valetta and, of particular importance, the Elgin Community. The Elgin Association for the Improvement of the Coloured People, under the leadership of Rev. William King, purchased 4,600 acres of the clergy reserves in the western part of Raleigh Township in 1849. The so-called Buxton settlement became a haven for self-emancipated slaves, and a model for community development from the very beginning.

Eventually mills were established, farms were cleared, schooling was begun, and communities began to thrive. In the early days, farmers and manufacturers took their yields and wares to the nearest dock on Lake Erie at Erieau, Coatsworth, and Buckhorn, or to the George Jacobs dock on the Thames. In the 1870s, the Canada Southern Railway came through, improving the prospects of villages like Cook's Corners, Merlin, and Tilbury. The Lake Erie and Detroit River Railway did the same for Wheatley in the 1890s.

Still, the land in the northern reaches of this quadrant of Kent County was deemed unusable for farming, or settling. The Raleigh Plain and adjacent lands in Tilbury East were underwater for at least a part of each year, and despite the soil being very fertile, these areas could not be farmed without being drained. By the late nineteenth century, there were men prepared to invest in the proper machinery. The first was the Martin Scoop waterwheel, which was utilized in Dover Township. In Raleigh, the Pike Drainage Scheme was put in place by John B. Pike in 1883. In Tilbury East, Henry Forbes was the man with the waterwheel. It took some tenacity, but by the early 1900s the lands in the northern reaches of southwest Kent were providing excellent crops, which they continue to do today.

One of the most exciting developments in the late 1800s in Southwest Kent was the discovery of oil and gas in what became known as the Tilbury Field. Men like the Coste brothers, A.T. Gurd, and John Kerr were the primary movers and shakers, exploring the fields and putting down oil drilling machines. In 1902, the famous "Gurd Gusher" was drilled in Raleigh, and Kerr No. 1 in Tilbury East hit oil a few years later. However, none of these wells produced much oil for very long, a disappointment until the use of natural gas—and the true potential of Tilbury Field—was discovered. In the early days, there were many small companies competing to both dig the wells and get the contracts to pipe natural gas into cities and towns. Eventually, in 1912, the Union Gas Company emerged as a main player in the natural gas industry.

Meanwhile, another invention would come to have a great effect on the economy of Southwest Kent: the automobile. Canadian Top Company (later the Canadian Top and Body), which first appeared in Tilbury in 1910, and Hudson Motors of Canada Limited became leading area employers, helping the community weather the Depression. Today, Tilbury still has a number of automotive parts plants.

The dawn of the twentieth century forced the citizens of southwest Kent to face the same issues as many others: they sent their young to war and they faced the prospect of little or no employment during the Depression years. However, they also enjoyed the pleasures that come from living in small communities where people look after each other. This strong community bond helped to protect them from the ups and downs of modern living and gave those of us who are living here today a solid foundation: a fine heritage to look back on.

St. Peter's Church in Tilbury East Township, the second oldest parish in western Ontario, started as a small log cabin chapel in 1802. After a second frame church burned in 1895, this brick church—seen here in the 1940s—was built. Although by that time most parishioners travelled by road, the church faces the river as a tribute to a time when transportation to Mass was by the Thames.

Within five months of Reverend William King establishing the settlement of Buxton with fifteen former slaves, they established a school, seen here circa 1910. At the start, the Mission School of the 1850s was the only school of its kind in North America to offer a classical education to Black students.

The community of Fletcher got its start because of the Canada Southern Railway and was named for John Fletcher, a teacher who gave the railway the land it needed for the station. Lumber was shipped in great quantities, and the Crewe brothers brought their fish from Port Crewe, on Lake Erie, to the station regularly. Oil and gas also fueled the economy of this small hamlet, but by the early twentieth century, it slipped into decline, gradually losing its commercial enterprises.

A Buxton teacher and students in front of the third one-room schoolhouse built on this spot. It was constructed in 1861 and operated as a school until 1968.

John Watkins' blacksmith shop was one of the first services in Buxton, established 1877. At the height of its growth, the Buxton Settlement's population topped 2000.

When Reverend William King and his financier Lord Elgin purchased 9000 acres of land in Raleigh Township for the utopian community of Buxton, they intended it to be free from alcohol. This Temperance Hotel helped to fulfill that mandate; it offered rooms and a place to socialize without selling alcohol. Built by Alfred West in the 1850s, the building was in a state of decline when this picture was taken in the 1920s.

This picture, taken circa 1908, shows a horse-drawn steam engine powering a grain threshing machine owned by Prince Chase, operated here on the farm of Fred Slade. As in most farm communities, the farmer who owned such an expensive harvesting machine would be hired by his neighbours to do their threshing.

Papa Prince's Pleasure Parlour was a café owned by Alpheus Prince, who was the postmaster in Buxton from 1923-4. Pictured here circa 1935, the business was indeed a café—despite what its name might suggest.

After the Emancipation Proclamation in America, many of the Black residents from the Buxton Settlement—now bearing a progressive education from the Buxton School—returned to their former homes in the southern United States. However, this picture of Buxton's main street, taken circa 1920, does not hint at the dramatic population decline.

Seen here circa 1900, the Canada Southern Railway began building tracks at the north end of the Buxton Settlement as part of its route from Fort Erie to the Detroit River in 1872.

The British Methodist Episcopal Church in Buxton was built between 1866 and 1872 and served as both the principle place of worship and final resting place for many residents. Throughout the years, the church has remained a sacred spot for the settlement's residents.

The Buxton girls' baseball team, circa 1920s. The team travelled as far as St. Thomas to play. According to the Buxton Museum, Muriel—the last girl on the right in the second row—outlived her teammates, and was 100 years old when she died.

This 550-pound bell was given to Reverend William King and his settlement in 1850 by the African American community in Pittsburgh. From that time forward, the bell was rung to celebrate the arrival of each new formerly enslaved refugee in Buxton. Today, the original bell, pictured here, hangs in the steeple of St. Andrew's United Church in South Buxton. An exact replica sits at the Buxton National Historic Site in North Buxton.

The community of North Buxton has always been good to all of its residents. The story accompanying these *Chatham Daily News* photographs from July 1946 tell of the fire that consumed Mrs. Henry Chase's home. All that was recovered was one chair, and one of 300 chickens. Everything else was lost. The eighty-year-old woman was living with neighbours, and the community had already banded together to start building her a new home.

This cairn was erected on River Road in Raleigh Township in 1936 to mark a skirmish in the War of 1812 in which thirty-seven Canadian militiamen boldly captured American soldiers bivouacked at the house of Thomas McCrae. The skirmish occurred in December 1813, two months after the Battle of the Thames.

This grand hotel in the community of Buckhorn was pre-dated by another less pretentious one called the Farmers' House, which displayed a set of buck's antlers on a tall pole, leading to the village's name of Buckhorn. Like many other settlements on the Talbot Road, Buckhorn thrived in the days before the railroad came, and it had a dock on Lake Erie for shipping goods.

The Methodist church in Charing Cross pictured here was first constructed in 1872, but a windstorm blew away two of its walls shortly after it was completed. It was rebuilt and opened in August 1873.

Barn raising on the Herb Smith farm, Cedar Springs, circa 1910.

In the late 1800s, "Buckhorn" was changed to "Cedar Springs." The mainstay industry in Cedar Springs is apples, as the local climate provides a longer growing season than the rest of Canada.

Pictured here in 1947, these local kids stand in front of a portrait of Harry Bedford Miner. Miner was born in Cedar Springs, the son of John and Orphra Miner. He died on the Western front, fighting the First World War with the 58th Battalion CEF. During the Hundred Days Offensive, he rushed an enemy machine-gun post, killing their crew and turning the gun onto the enemy, all while severely wounded. He was posthumously awarded the Victoria Cross for bravery—the British Empire's highest military honour and the only one awarded to a soldier from Chatham-Kent.

The Coatsworth family came to the Romney Township lakeshore in the 1920s and built the brick house still known as the Coatsworth house in 1828 on Talbot Road. The original settlement grew up around a dock put in by Caleb Coatsworth in the early 1870s. According to Victor Lauriston, the dock was destroyed by an iceburg in 1895. The settlement then moved to the railroad, where this mill was built.

The settlement at the crossroads of the Harwich/Raleigh Townline (County Road 10) and the Middle Road (Hwy 98) was first called Cook's Corners, after an English settler who arrived around 1830. By the time the Canada Southern Railway came to the community in 1874, the settlement was renamed Charing Cross. The trains would stop here and some passengers would transfer to Chatham, first by stage, and after 1908, by the Chatham, Wallaceburg, and Lake Erie electric line, pictured here.

This picture purports to be of the first combine in Ontario, taken at Rendall Farms in Coatsworth.

Metropolitan Opera star Jeanne "Ruby" Gordon built this home on sixteen acres of wooded ravine and parkland in 1930. After her death, the house was opened to the public as a hotel in August 1947, only to be hampered by the fact that Raleigh Township was a "dry" township.

A typical dredge cut and dike near Jeannettes Creek Station on the GTR, 1913. This area is most known for a train wreck that occurred at Baptiste Creek, near Jeannettes Creek, on the Great Western Railway in 1854. In foggy conditions, a passenger train collided with a heavy-laden gravel train. According to reports, the second-class cars, carrying immigrants en route to Windsor, were "smashed into bits and pieces." The number of dead totaled fifty-two, with dozens more injured.

The lighthouse seen here, near the mouth of the Thames River, is the second oldest lighthouse still standing in Ontario. It was built in 1818, after the original lighthouse was burned during the War of 1812. The Cartier family, purported to be descendants of explorer Jacques Cartier, tended this light for about 130 years until Dick Cartier died in 1950.

Loading sugarbeets at Jeannettes Creek CPR Station, 1913. A brochure appearing in England in the early 1900s, put out by the CPR, promised immigrants ten acres of land and a house in "Jeannette." Families like the Kings took advantage; their descendants still live in the area today. So did the Beardall family, and their son, Jack, went on to establish CFCO Radio in Chatham.

Another iconic sight on the southern bank of the Thames, at its mouth, is the Lighthouse Inn. Built in 1947 by Armand and Vera Jacobs as a place for duck hunters and fishermen to stay, the inn became popular for its perch dinners. It was torn down in 2018.

Merlin suffered at least two major fires, including the one pictured here in 1908. The fire swept through the developing village's business district and wiped out the *Merlin Mirror* newspaper offices, A.W. Smith's Jewellery Store, and the Brethor's Barber Shop. It also spread to the IOOF Lodge, to the right of the fire in this photo.

Known at the time for its distinctive striped awnings, the Sales and Halliday Block in Merlin dates back to 1915. A one-stop shopping destination, the block was destroyed by fire one year later.

After the Merlin Continuation School burned to the ground in 1942, there was a need to find temporary quarters for the pupils. The United Church was used to house the elementary students, but the town had no choice but to set up the continuation students in the old Marquis Hotel, seen here, where bathrooms, dining rooms, and kitchens were used as classrooms. This arrangement continued until 1948.

It took seven years to build a new high school in Merlin because the school board was waiting for approval to build a "district" school—a new concept at the time. When the Merlin District High School was built in 1948, it was the first district school in the province.

In 1877, James Marshall, along with his two sons, John and George, brought steam-powered saw and grist mills to Merlin, seen here in the early 1900s.

This school, the original school in Merlin, was built in 1879. By 1910, the Merlin Public and Continuation School had elementary students on the first floor and secondary students on the second, until the building was consumed by fire in 1942.

Located on the main corner of town, J.C. "Chick" Dent's Garage always attracted a crowd. This mainstay in Merlin endured for fifty-seven years.

Little is known about this canning factory, other than its short life span. The British Canadian Canners Limited constructed a number of buildings, as seen here in this 1914 postcard. However, the town well water rusted the cans too quickly and the Merlin village council refused to put in a water line from the lake to solve the problem. As a result, the canning company ceased operations beside the railroad tracks on Stanley Street in 1916.

Although Port Alma was named for an early postmaster's wife, this small fishing port of Lake Erie only developed into a village when the natural gas plant was established there in 1913. To secure a fair share of gas from the Tilbury gas fields, a compressor plant was built here. The building on the left was a boarding house.

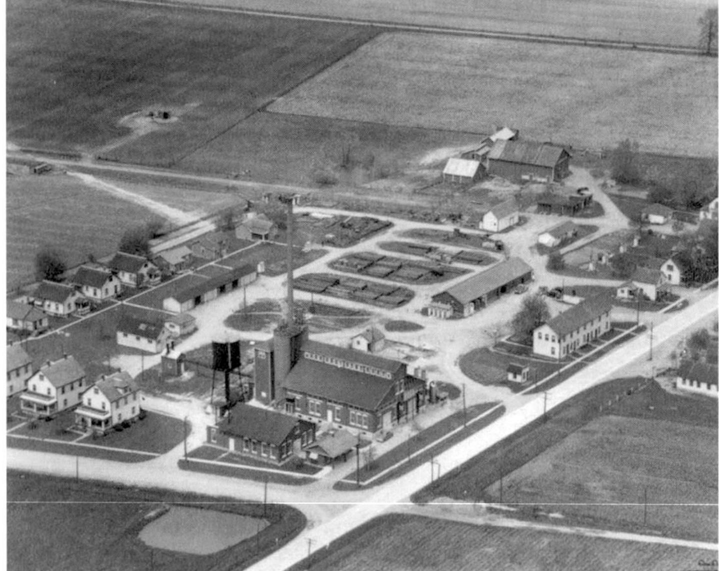

This aerial photo taken in 1947 shows the full extent of the carefully planned Port Alma complex. The plant itself, the gas company offices, and workers' residences are all visible. In 1980, Union Gas sold the facilities.

According to older residents, Presley's Service Station in Alma was the place where "the world's problems were solved." It was also the spot where kids could endlessly "ride their bikes around the track behind the garage" and, according to more than one former frequenter, you could "even get a shot of rye whisky!"

In the 1890s, Merlin was booming. Oil and natural gas wells had been discovered in nearby Raleigh Township, Marshall's Grist and Stave Mill opened, and the first telephone system was installed. The Lake Erie Detroit Railway also came to town, connecting Merlin to a line that ran from Ridgetown to Leamington.

Opening day for the Prarie Siding Bridge, October 25, 1925. The one-armed ferryman, Alex Reaume, was given the job as bridge keeper, in gratitude for his many years of service.

The small farming community of Prairie Siding grew up in the early 1900s between the Thames River and the railroad. The general store closest to the railway line was called "Soup's" and it is pictured here in this sketch by Elsie Thoonen. "Soup" Johnston, a jovial man, ran the store, which also acted as an unofficial community centre.

James S. Richardson store, circa 1910, Tilbury. John Richardson established a successful pearlash factory around 1853, using wood from his farm. In 1875, when the Canada Southern Railway came through the area, he opened this store for his son, James, who developed it into one of the largest stores in Tilbury.

The Grand Central Hotel was built, as its name suggests, in the centre of Tilbury in 1887. The three storey brick hotel contained twenty-one bedrooms, and was owned, after 1890, by George McKay. Key to the hotel's success was its location on the west side of Queen Street, Tilbury's main thoroughfare and the county line between Essex and Kent counties. The west side of the street was wet, allowing for alcohol sales, while the east side was dry.

Laying the cornerstone of St. Francis Xavier Church, 1894. In the early days, Tilbury's Roman Catholics had to travel to St. Peter's Church on the Thames. In 1855, they were finally able to worship in their own church on Middle Road, a ways outside town. Finally, in 1894, the current St. Francis Xavier church was built, despite the objections of a vocal minority of parishioners, who wanted the new church built on the original site.

In 1887, most Anglicans were attending service in Comber, and they discouraged the new Reverend, Thomas Dobson, from coming to town. Undaunted, by 1901, he managed to see the construction of the new St. Andrew's Church in Tilbury. He remained there for 50 years. In 1918, the congregation surprised him with a new car which he promptly crashed into a bridge! It was soon fixed and he used it for many years.

At the turn of the century, scores of drillers and operators descended on Tilbury in search of oil. While the oil dwindled, speculators found a use for the natural gas, creating a lasting part of Tilbury's economy.

The school featured in this 1925 photograph was the product of a partnership: the land was purchased by Dominion Gas, the school building was funded by Union Gas, and the teacher was hired and paid by the local parents. This arrangement lasted until the school was incorporated into the local school section.

In 1921, many farmers bought shares in Gove Motor Company and watched the company begin construction on a large factory on the southern outskirts of town. When Gove abandoned its unfinished factory, their backers suffered a major financial blow.

E.G. Odette came to Tilbury in 1910 and founded the Canadian Top Company (later the Canadian Top and Body), which he owned and managed until 1934—while holding political office as Mayor from 1921-3 and as MP for Essex East.

Hudson Essex, later Hudson Motors of Canada, Limited, began assembling cars in Tilbury in 1932, using the factory that had been abandoned by the Gove Motor Company. The company was retooled for wartime production and remained an important contributor to Tilbury's prosperity until it left for Toronto in the 1950s.

W.C. Crawford came to Tilbury Centre in 1885. He took over the Powell Brothers' store and built the Crawford Block to house it. The business grew into one of Southwestern Ontario's best department stores, aptly called the "Big Store." He also established Crawford's Handle Factory, one of the largest of its kind in Canada, before turning to a life in municipal politics.

The Canadian Top and Body Company remained one of Tilbury's main employers throughout the 1930s and 1940s. The company assembled both the Essex and Terraplane cars for the Hudson Motors Co. before being retooled for the Second World War, when production shifted to mechanical transports and CMPs for the Royal Canadian Army. In 1947, control of Canadian Top and Body passed to Chatco Steel Products of Chatham.

In 1908, Prime Minister Wilfrid Laurier kicked off his election campaign on September 21 before a crowd of 10,000. The *Toronto Daily Star* put it best: "Tilbury had flags and bunting from head to foot. Tilbury had arches of evergreen. Tilbury had decorations more or less elaborate on nearly every business block."

This picture of Fordson tractors outside the Richardson's Ford business calls to mind the story of James Fletcher. He was an area farmer who went to Ford headquarters in Dearborn, Michigan, after seeing an ad for forthcoming Fordson Tractors. Once there, a secretary directed him to Henry Ford, who was working out in the yard with his son Edsel. James recommended that Fordson tractors need a pulley attachment—which Ford promised he was working on and would deliver by July. At the end of the summer, the $65 pulley attachment was sent to Mr. Fletcher, at no charge, because of the delay. At right, a Fordson tractor demonstration shows off the 1921 model.

Mrs. Loma Phaneuf (nee Reaume) started teaching in the Tilbury area at sixteen, but she always had an aptitude for design and construction. After her husband died, she was forced to support her family, leading her to build her own house and then become a real estate developer.

Loma Phaneuf acquired and managed the Balmoral Hotel in Tilbury. She also built and ran the Star Theatre for many years, going so far as to acquire contracts with Hollywood film companies to show first-run movies to Tilbury residents. In a *Saturday Night* profile of Loma published in 1913, the writer gushed, "She is doing work which few men and not one woman in a thousand could accomplish, quietly, and thoroughly."

Early views of Queen Street, Tilbury. There is still a dirt street, but the presence of hydro poles indicates the arrival of electricity to town. The plank sidewalk stretched from the Canadian Pacific Railroad to the Middle Road. Mungo Stewart's Hardware is also visible.

The Bell Telephone system came to Tilbury in 1913. By 1936, its switchboard was in the Foster block, operated by the women seen here, known as the Tilbury Belles. A true community service, the Belles connected calls, operated as emergency dispatch, and were even known to hand-deliver important messages when phone lines were down.

The eccentric George R. Bromley served as president of the Patriotic Junk Association in Tilbury during the Second World War, collecting scrap for the war effort with his horse and cart.

A group of boys watch the Palmer Block on Queen Street in downtown Tilbury go up in flames in 1903.

The Empire Hotel in Tilbury was established in the early 1900s by Joseph Peltier, one of the first settlers to the townsite. In 1907, Peltier retired and sold the Empire to his son-in-law, Barnaby Ballard. The Ballards ran the Empire Hotel until 1948. The Empire was the first hotel to receive its liquor licence after Prohibition ended in 1934.

The Commercial Hotel in Wheatley, pictured here (circa 1896) on "The Glorious 12th." According to reports, some 8,000 people came to the village only to be interrupted by a torrential downpour. The Commercial Hotel fell victim to fire on February 25, 1901, burning in less than thirty minutes.

The Tilbury East Farmers' Club Corn Wheel, shown here at the Essex Farm Show, was created to promote the growing of corn, which in 1913 was not a prominent area crop. Two of the men in the picture, James and John Fletcher, had seen the newly invented Ferris wheel at the Louisiana Purchase Exposition in St. Louis in 1904, the inspiration for their own wheel of corn.

The Lanoue family stands in front of their home, likely the oldest still standing in Tilbury. The Lanoue House was built for Stephen Gervais on the northwest corner of Canal and Queen streets (where the post office now sits) circa 1855—although local tradition suggests it was built by Joseph L'Arche. Jean-Baptiste Lanoue moved the house to its current location at 20 Canal Street W. in 1865 and covered the logs with clapboard. Today, it is preserved as a heritage home.

This view of Talbot Road, taken on the eastern outskirts of the village circa 1900, shows the Wheatley Flour Mill, which had been established about twenty years previously just across the creek.

Wheatley's other main street is (confusingly) called Lake Street, Main Street, and Erie Street. The building in the left foreground, located on the southeast corner, is the IOOF Building, where the Union Bank of Canada had its office in 1906. The intersection of Main Street with Talbot Road, the main corner in the village, can be seen beyond that block on the left.

This staged shot along the railroad in Tilbury East township was taken in 1906. Judging by the land on either side of the railroad bed, it was probably taken in the northern reaches of the township, a swamp which was only then being drained.

On January 15, 1936, a gas leak caused a tremendous explosion at the corner of Main Street and Elm Street in Wheatley. A few minutes later, nothing remained of the IOOF Building but rubble. Thankfully, the explosion occurred around 1:30 a.m., so the only people slightly injured were two women walking home from a party.

A.B. Lounsbury established this butcher shop near the southeast corner of Erie and Talbot Streets in 1883. Close inspection of the picture reveals that the building is supported by wooden blocks or pegs. The earliest name for the community was "Pegtown," because so many of the buildings were supported by pegs like these. William Buchanan, who did not like the name, which was sometimes changed to "Pigtown," applied for a post office named "Wheatley" after his late father-in-law, Richard Wheatley, a pioneer settler.

This 1940 photo reveals the challenges faced by fishermen before the government built a proper harbour. Boats would either have to be drawn up on hoists or pulled up onto the beach. This problem was ameliorated in 1951 when Wheatley Harbour was officially opened.

Before refrigeration, the only way for fishermen to preserve their catch was to harvest ice from the lake during the winter. This photo shows part of the process. The ice was cut up and put into a boat, then brought to the shore. A pulley system allowed the fishermen to move the ice up the bank and into the icehouse. The ice was stored underground, and covered with sawdust, within the icehouse.

In 1904, this attractive brick school was built on Lamarsh Street in Wheatley. The former school was moved closer to the lake, giving the village two public schools. Unfortunately, this building was destroyed by fire on February 2, 1943, just after the students had been dismissed for the day. Because the war was on, the school could not be rebuilt, so the students were housed throughout the village, some at the continuation school.

The community of Wheatley was formed around the mouth of two creeks, which formed the eastern boundary of the village. Two Creeks was also the name of a proposed, but never built, canal to take all Great Lakes shipping from Lake Erie to Lake St. Clair, beginning at Two Creeks and ending near Jeannettes Creek.

The boat wreck seen here is the fishing tug R&G, which went down in October 1941, with a loss of four lives. Not fishing but charted that day, twenty-five-year-old R.G. McLean skippered the boat, aided by T.I. Epplett. They were taking Mrs. Charles Aubrey and her son to Pelee Island to negotiate the purchase of a hotel there.

The building in this picture, located about nine miles east of Wheatley on Lake Erie, began as the Detroit Police Country Club in the 1920s. Unfortunately, the money ran out before the building was finished and the building fell into the hands of its mortgage holder, Milton Crewe. Weekly dances were held in the ballroom, unfinished but still usable. Around 1948, the building was leased to the Pentecostal Assembly and rechristened the Wheatley Convention Hall. It burned in 1960.

Erie Street, looking north, Wheatley, 1910. On the right of the intersection, across Talbot Road, is the E. Hanson general store, which had been expanded a few years earlier. The left corner is taken up with E. Omstead's general store, which he had acquired in 1906 from the Whitney Brothers.

In 1932, the Wheatley Band was revived and the Wheatley Community Club soon started holding summer concerts in the park. Under bandmaster Ivan Coulter, the band started winning competitions across Ontario and Michigan. The concerts even got a mention in *Maclean's* magazine, which complimented the village on its efforts.

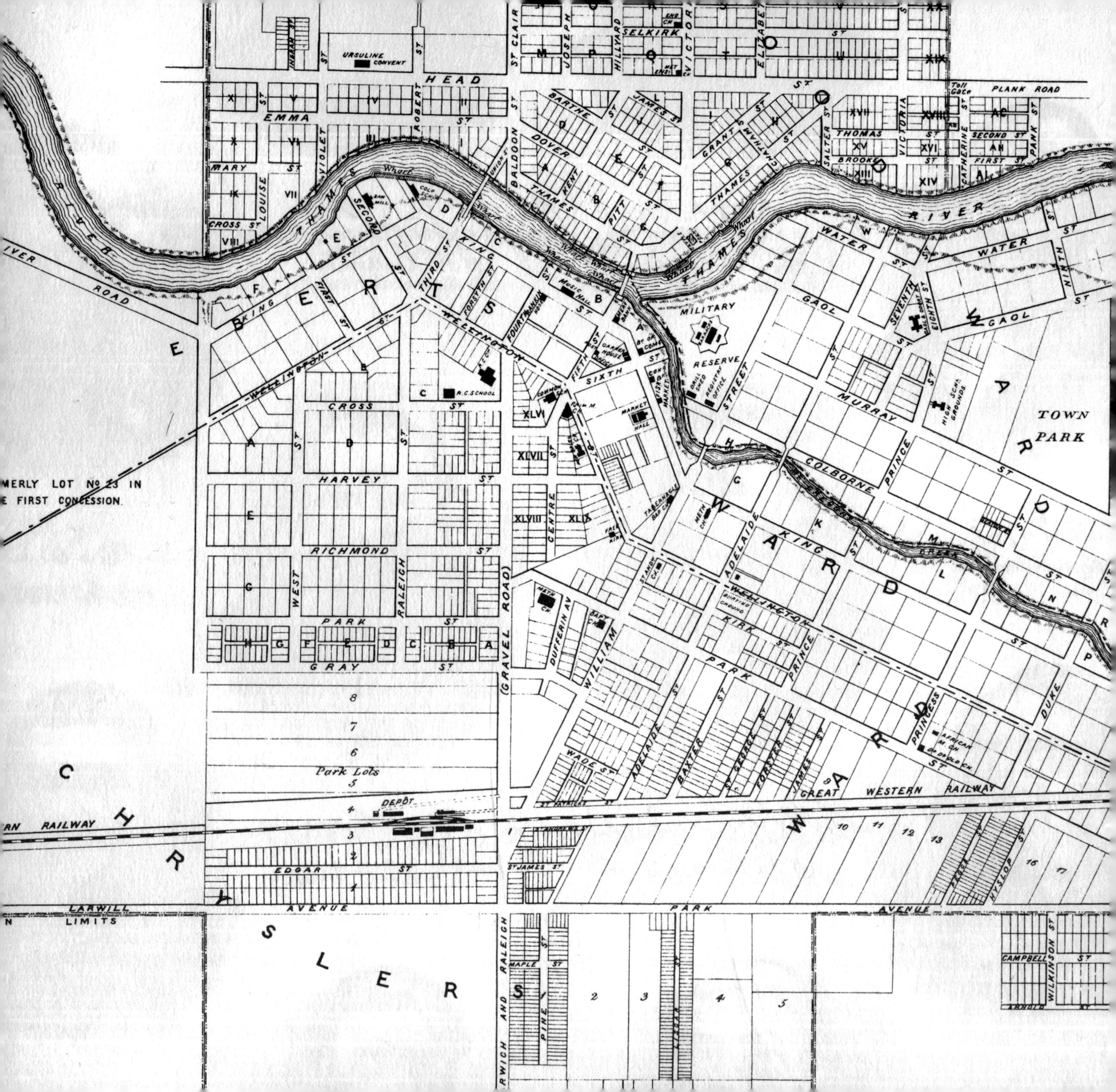
URSULINE CONVENT
HEAD ST
ST CLAIR
JOSEPH
HILLYARD
SELKIRK
VICTORIA
ELIZABETH
EMMA ST
ROBERT ST
MARY ST
VIOLET
LOUISE
CROSS ST
THAMES
Wharf
SAW MILL
COL'D SCH
UNION ST
BALDOON ST
BARTHE
DOVER
KENT
PITT
JAMES ST
GRANT
CHATHAM
SALTER ST
THOMAS
BROOKE
SECOND ST
FIRST ST
CATHERINE
PARK
PLANK ROAD
Toll Gate
RIVER
THAMES RIVER
RIVER ROAD
KING ST
FIRST
SECOND
THIRD ST
FORSYTH ST
FOURTH
WELLINGTON
FIFTH ST
SIXTH
Music Hall
MILITARY
RESERVE
WATER ST
GAOL ST
SEVENTH
EIGHTH ST
NINTH
MURRAY
HIGH SCH. GROUNDS
TOWN PARK
R.C. CH
R.C.SCHOOL
CROSS ST
HARVEY ST
RICHMOND ST
PARK ST
GRAY ST
WEST ST
RALEIGH ST
CENTRE
(GRAVEL ROAD)
MARKET HALL
DRILL SHED
REGISTRY OFFICE
STREET
COLBORNE
PRINCE
MCGREGOR CREEK
KING ST
WELLINGTON
TABERNACLE BAP. CH
METH CH
BURYING GROUND
KIRK ST
PARK ST
DUFFERIN AV
WILLIAM
ADELAIDE
BAXTER ST
ST GEORGE ST
FORSTER ST
JAMES ST
WADE ST
PRINCESS
AFRICAN M. CH
DUKE
ST PATRICKS ST
GREAT WESTERN RAILWAY
FORMERLY LOT No 23 IN THE FIRST CONCESSION
Park Lots
DEPÔT
RAILWAY
EDGAR ST
ST ANDREWS ST
ST JAMES ST
LARWILL AVENUE
PARK AVENUE
LIMITS
NORWICH AND RALEIGH
MAPLE ST
PINE
HYSLOP ST
CAMPBELL ST
WILKINSON ST
ARNOLD ST
ROBERTS WARD
CHRYSLERS
WARD
WARD
WARD

CHAPTER FIVE
Chatham

Sir John Graves Simcoe's plans for the defense of Upper Canada in the 1790s included the future township of Chatham. Simcoe also gave the place its name. Always conscious of the threat posed by the new American state just to the southwest, Simcoe believed the site would make a good naval depot, just like Chatham in England, along its own Thames River. The landmark was an important navigation point for large boats on the Canadian Thames, and the river led to a vast fresh water route, the Great Lakes.

As soon as he got the chance, Simcoe made a trip to the Thames. When he and his party passed the future Chatham in the winter of 1793, his secretary Major E.B. Littlehales noted in his journal, that they, "...reconnoitred a fork in the River, and examined a mill of curious construction erecting upon it." This mill had been built by Thomas Clarke, a Loyalist who had settled on the Thames before Patrick McNiff made his first survey of the river in 1791. The mill was indeed curious, as Clarke had not bothered to trim the logs at each end of the walls. The mill would eventually came into the hands of Clarke's creditor, John McGregor, who gave his name to the nearby creek.

Abraham Iredell, the deputy-surveyor for the Western District, plotted the townsite of Chatham by order of Simcoe in August 1795. Iredell decided to build a cabin there, at the corner of William and Water Streets, and it was he who became Chatham's first permanent resident. He may be buried in present-day Tecumseh Park, where it is believed he died in 1806.

Iredell was not immediately joined by a wave of settlers. William Chrysler arrived and began farming along the river, near the northwest corner of King and Third Streets, in 1820. Other individuals arrived in the years that followed, but the settlement was not firmly established until after the Upper Canada Rebellion of 1837. In response to the uprising, the government of Upper Canada brought a military presence to several settlements, including fledging Chatham. They built a complex with barracks on the military reserve Iredell had laid out. The military presence heightened the economic and social fabric of the settlement, and was soon followed by municipal self-rule and the creation of Kent County as a county separate from Essex, with Chatham named as its capital in 1849. Other businesses and industries were arriving, with shipbuilding emerging as Chatham's first important manufacturing concern.

Chatham's economic importance was sealed in 1854 when the Great Western Railway came to town. Only one year later, Chatham achieved town status. The original wooden store buildings and pioneer manufacturing complexes were being replaced by more substantial brick edifices, and Chatham's halcyon days were in full swing.

The carriage works established by William Gray in 1856 was continued by his son Robert after William's untimely death in 1884. Robert was a forward thinker and in 1915 launched Gray-Dort Motors, Ltd. in affiliation with Dallas Dort, of Flint, Michigan. This became one of the most successful early car companies in Canada, but its growth potential was thwarted by Dort's resignation in 1921. Unable to continue on his own, he was forced to close—a blow not only to the 800 employees of the company, but to the city.

A similar enterprise began as the D.R. Van Allen sawmill in 1858 on Head Street East (Grand Avenue). By 1882, Van Allen foresaw the decline of his shipbuilding operation and moved to form the Chatham Manufacturing Company. The company made farm wagons, and good ones too. When the International Harvester Company placed an order for 2000 wagons in 1904, they were so impressed with the product that they decided to buy the whole company. International Harvester went on to become one of Chatham's most important employers throughout the twentieth century and into the next.

Another important company established in the late 1800s in Chatham was the T.H. Taylor Flour and Woollen Mills. The woollen business was discontinued in 1923, but the flour milling service remained in operation until it was sold to Dover Industries. Another business which became nationally famous for a time was the Manson Campbell Fanning Mill factory, which, around the turn of the twentieth century, was turning out 10,000 fanning mills (used to thresh grain) a year. The Park Brothers' Foundry also enjoyed high repute, making engines and boilers, and doing sheet-iron work.

Chatham was not just a manufacturing town. It also aspired to mercantile importance and valued cultural improvement. The Chatham Market was considered to be the best small-town market in Ontario. At the centre of a vast, fertile agricultural region, Chatham's market stalls overflowed with the bounty of the fields. Other large business concerns were the Charles Austin Department Store, the New York House grocery owned by Hugh Malcolmson, and the Hotel Sanita, a mineral springs hotel located where the present-day Chatham Cultural Centre sits.

Educational and cultural pursuits were not neglected either. Scane's Music Hall, on King Street, between Fourth and Fifth Streets, housed a theatre within its five-storey building which could seat 1200 people. It was the setting for some of the best travelling acts of the time, including Jenny Lind and the Marx Brothers. The Canada Business College was another institution that enjoyed a good reputation. Located for many years at various places on King Street (where one of its students was Tom Thomson), its proprietor, Duncan McLachlin, built a massive new building on William Street in 1905.

Chatham produced its share of famous cultural figures as well. Geoffrey O'Hara, an important songwriter, and Arthur Stringer, a well-known writer, both grew up in the city. Marie Dressler, the silent movie star, went to McKeough School in the 1900s, and A.M. Fleming, the accomplished landscape painter who kept a studio on King Street for many years, spent his formative years on a farm just outside Chatham as well.

Chatham started the twentieth century on a high, with the anticipation of years of continued prosperity to come. And yet, like most other places, Chatham received an unwelcome wake-up call in the First World War. Many of its best and brightest young men went away to "the war to end all wars" and never came back, or came back much changed in body and mind. Chathamites came to realize that they were not immune to the influence of the outside world—for good or ill.

The years of the Great Depression drove home this point. While Kent's rich agricultural lands continued to provide the bounty they always had, many people still did not have the money to purchase enough food for their families. The Second World War also came to Chatham in a big way, with the establishment of the No.12 Canadian (Basic) Training Centre. As had happened in the 1830s, the presence of the military helped improve Chatham's economic status, the community endured war-time rationing, and the dreaded news that their sons/brothers/husbands were not coming home. When V-E Day was finally celebrated on May 8, 1945, Chatham, like many other communities, was ready to forget the many years of want and embrace the future. The modern world had arrived.

In 1850, Martin R. Delaney became the first Black man admitted to Harvard Medical School. Becoming a doctor and a leading abolitionist, he moved to Chatham in 1856. In 1858, he sailed for Africa to explore potential sites for a Black republic. Returning to Chatham in 1860, he soon left again for the United States to recruit Black men for the Union Army, becoming himself a surgeon for the famed 54th Massachusetts regiment. Today, Delaney is remembered as a father of Black nationalism.

This view of Sixth Street, looking towards McGregor's Creek, was painted by Lieutenant Philip John Bainbrigge in 1838 during his travels in Upper Canada. Chatham was very much a frontier village at this time.

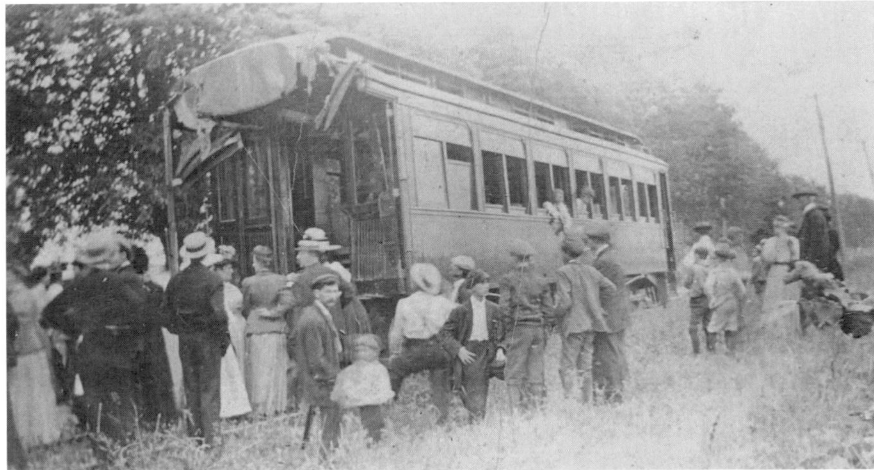

On August 10, 1908, a civic holiday, two overcrowded train cars on the Chatham, Wallaceburg and Lake Erie Railway left the station at King Street and William Street for Erie Beach. Car 14 stopped to pick up another passenger, just opposite the fairgrounds on Queen Street when Car 8, which had been following too closely, rammed into it, knocking many passengers (who were crammed onto the back landing) onto the tracks. Four people were killed in what was known as Black Monday in Chatham.

The Legary Bakery was situated on Park Avenue E. in Chatham. In its heyday, the bakery employed five expert bakers and was known as "the quality baker in town." The Legary delivery wagon is pictured here, circa 1920.

The Royal Exchange Hotel, located on the southwest corner of King and Fifth streets and built in 1841, was Chatham's most palatial hotel for more than twenty years. The building was begun by Joseph Northwood but finished by William and Walter Eberts, three giants of industry in early Chatham. It was called "the largest hotel west of Toronto," and it remained an important gathering place until February 15, 1898, when it succumbed to fire after a Valentine's Day dance, on the coldest night of the year.

Chatham's first post office, established in the early 1830s, was on John McGregor's farm, situated beyond the end of King Street East. McGregor was an important early grist mill owner. His mill burned down in 1813.

The Dowsley Spring and Axle Company began business on St. George Street, just south of the Grand Trunk Railway tracks in 1902. It manufactured springs and axles for the new horseless carriages, and as such, it became Chatham's first automotive parts factory. The company merged with Ontario Steel in 1913.

Harvesting ice blocks on the Thames River, circa 1902.

The Excelsior Fire Brigade poses on the west side of the Chatham Market Square, with their fire engines behind them, for a group portrait in 1876.

The War of 1812 commercial schooner General Myers was found at the bottom of the Thames River, just west of the CPR Railroad bridge, in 1900. They believed it was a vessel burned by the British army during their less-than-orderly retreat up the river in the fall of 1813. It was displayed in Tecumseh Park, as seen here.

The Tecumseh Historical Society hoped to build a museum around the General Myers, but when funds never materialized, the craft was broken up and various wooden pieces—including this couch—were made from it. In modern times, it was determined that the craft was actually the commercial schooner *Miamis*, which burned at the same time in 1813.

Chatham's first scout troop, 1912.

The Canada Business College, founded by Duncan McLachlan in 1876, was one of the first schools of shorthand and business training in the country. When enrolment continued to rise, a new College—seen here in an early postcard—opened in 1906 on Queen Street, formerly the site of a baseball diamond. On that spot, on June 2, 1898, Rube Waddell led Chatham in the famous game against the Page Fence Giants in front of 1200 fans. They lost.

A "cyclone" came through Chatham on June 8, 1906. It took down several of the city's iconic maple trees, as well as a large flagpole in Tecumseh Park, before demolishing the Park Street Methodist Church's lofty steeple. This photo shows the damage just a few blocks away from the church, on Centre Street.

In May 1860, Mother Mary Francis Xavier Le Bihan and another Ursuline nun established a school at the corner of Wellington and First streets, but within a year the school had already outgrown the premises. In 1866, the Ursuline sisters purchased twelve acres of Dr. Pegley's estate, fronting on Head Street (Grand Avenue). There they founded "The Pines," a complex that included this chapel, built in 1899, which served the sisters until it was replaced in the early 1960s.

Noted abolitionist Mary Ann Shadd Cary was the first Black woman in North America to publish a newspaper, *The Provincial Freeman*. She moved to Chatham for several years in the 1850s, joining a group of Black intellectuals.

Duncan McLachlan, the founder of the popular Canada Business College, built this home on William Street South in the 1870s. This early 1900s photograph shows his extended family, likely including his son Kent, who would leave Chatham for Hollywood and become a popular film star known as Keene Duncan.

C&D Sugar silos, 1950. The Dominion Sugar Company opened a new refinery in Chatham in 1916, on a sixty-four-acre property just east of Merritt Avenue. It soon became the national headquarters for the Canada and Dominion Sugar Company, after its merger with the Canada Sugar Refining Company (Redpath) at the end of 1930.

An early view of Thames Street in Chatham, taken from the Fifth Street Bridge. Dominion Stores Ltd. and the Bluebird Tea Room are visible, as is Martin's Meat Market to the left—albeit under construction by Frank Sparks. This block burned down on June 3, 1972.

In the late 1870s, a group of concerned citizens, including journalist W.E. Hamilton, convinced Chatham Council to build a Home of the Friendless. They built this house in 1881. This *Chatham Daily News* image shows a fire at the home in 1946; thankfully, they did rebuild.

In April 1937, four days of almost continuous rain led the Thames to flood, affecting all the communities along its course, including Chatham. Here, onlookers look at the rising tide from the Fifth Street Bridge. In the city, the crest came on April 29, at 20 feet, 4 inches. It took out the Rankin Dock at the foot of Fourth Street and only heroic efforts prevented the Waterworks on Grand Avenue E. from being inundated with flood water.

This flood in March 1904 was, at its peak, likely only a few inches lower than the great flood of 1937. The waters crossed King Street downtown, schools were cancelled, and people resorted to boats to escape their homes. In the words of one diarist, "The greatest flood in thirty years sweeps on and on."

Ten years after the "worst flood in Chatham's history," another heavy rainfall in 1947 precipitated the second great flooding of the Thames. As this aerial photo suggests, the downtown area was once again affected, but King Street managed to stay above water. Areas north of the river were hardest hit.

During the flood in 1947, the *Chatham Daily News* needed to get its reporters in and out of the flooded area at the northern end of the Fifth Street Bridge. The paper decided to charter a special "Flood Ferry," seen here, for its workers and the public. At peak times, 400 people an hour climbed onto the bus, whose wheels and engine were high enough to stay out of the water and carry them across the bridge.

Abraham Iredell's initial survey of 1795 included provision for a market, which was duly established once settlement began in earnest in the 1840s. Seen here (from the rear) in the late 1800s, Chatham's market was one of the most famous in Ontario. The market, with the police station in the foreground and town hall visible at the other end of the market, have all been demolished.

A rare, early view of the Chatham Market. The police station had not yet been built at the Wellington Street end of the block.

Officer W.S. Donaldson of the Chatham police force was quite the motorcyclist. He was famous for being able to stop a runaway horse and wagon while riding his motorcycle. At right, his wife (donning his uniform) gives their daughter a ticket.

In 1855, the Chatham Grammar School was erected on Prince Street, where the Chatham Collegiate Institute building—now housing Darul Uloom Canada—stands today. By the late 1870s, it was being called the Chatham High School, and in 1887 it attained the coveted collegiate status.

By 1856, the Head Street School in north Chatham had over 100 students. It was moved to Forest Street in 1881 and became McKeough School to honour William McKeough, a popular school board chairman. The school seen here was built in the 1890s and lasted almost a century before being demolished.

Natural gas was discovered in Kent County in 1902. The Chatham Gas Company, with headquarters on King Street W. (site of today's Civic Centre), quickly became a leading competitor. In 1906, they partnered the Volcanic Oil and Gas Company and supplied Chatham with natural gas from the Halliday well, located just north of Fletcher. This company evolved into Union Natural Gas Company of Canada Ltd. in 1911.

This perspective of King Street was taken from the top of the CW&LE powerhouse chimney some time after 1905. The post office and customs building (centre, right) at the corner of Fourth Street was erected in 1884, while Harrison Hall and First Presbyterian Church were constructed in the 1890s. The Chatham Opera House stands on the river side of King Street, between Fourth and Fifth Streets (top right).

The upper bend of King Street in the 1930s, the heyday of the business district. The William Pitt Hotel, Spencer Stone department store, and the Brisco Hotel on the Scane block are all visible in this photograph.

Downtown Chatham, 1940s. The most prominent building, right of centre, is the Victoria Block, which was built by Isobel Garner. The Richardsonian Romanesque turrets of the three buildings—Harrison Hall, Central School, and First Presbyterian Church—can be seen in the distance.

In 1872, when the Canada Southern Railroad was finally built through this area, many Chathamites were disappointed that the line ran six miles south of the town. When the CPR arrived in 1888, they rectified the error, running the track through the middle of town. This station was designed by famed architect Bruce Price and stood at the eastern edge of the downtown until the 1980s.

The CPR Hotel, seen here in 1920, did not stand for Canadian Pacific Railway as one might guess. Instead, due to the train company's objections, the hotel was cleverly named the Chatham Pool and Recreation Hotel. The CPR Hotel anchored that end of King Street from 1890 until 1957, when a devastating fire in the building killed four people.

This King Street photograph looks east from the downtown area where many people of African descent settled in the 1840s and 1850s, when Chatham was known as a mecca for Black intellectuals. By the time of this photo, however, most of them had left.

During the Second World War, Chatham turned over a large tract of land south of the CNR tracks to the military for training. The No. 12 Canadian (Basic) Training Centre opened in October 1941 and was first used for army reserves. The training camp was converted to active service in February 1941 and grew into an extensive camp, extending from Willomac Avenue to beyond Tweedsmuir Street and from Queen Street to Lacroix Street, that could house some 1000 men.

A queue at the Griffin Theatre, 1919. Originally constructed as Bright's Opera House, the movie house was located at 55 King Street W., just opposite the east end of Market Square. At the time, tickets were twenty-five cents apiece.

Hydro workers climb up a pole just outside the Post Office on Fourth Street in 1914. They are likely preparing the city for hydroelectricity, which arrived the following year.

In 1900, the Chatham Mineral Water Company was formed to cash in on fashionable mineral bath spas and to sell the mineral water that had been found in a well on the McGregor farm just east of the city. By 1902, the company erected a bath house at the northeast corner of William Street N. and Murray Street, where T.H. Taylor had formerly lived (pictured at left). Inviting patrons to be treated by the healing waters, the venture was initially quite successful and by 1905, the house was converted into Hotel Sanita, pictured at right. Unfortunately, the mineral water in the well quickly dried up, and the company was forced to truck mineral water from Mount Clemens, Michigan. That expense, coupled with the troubles of Prohibition, led the company to file for bankruptcy. The City of Chatham snatched up the property at a bargain.

Two views of an early Presbyterian church in Chatham. At left, the church—built in the 1840s—is shown in its early days. At right, construction begins on the boarded-up, rundown church building in May 1947. The site would become M.J. Smith Seed Co. and was only recently demolished.

The Aberdeen Hotel stood at the southwest corner of Grand Avenue and St. Clair Street, seen here in the 1900s. It was originally established as the McNaughton Tavern in the late 1840s. The building still stands and is being used for storage by Western Equipment, which has its shop next door on St. Clair.

The Chatham Vocational School opened in 1924 on the former premises of the Hotel Sanita. The Ministry of Education had allowed the city to take over the hotel building on the condition that they either build a new school in the next five years or renovate the hotel. They chose the latter, and in 1926, a gymnasium and an auditorium were built around the corner on Murray Street.

In 1793, Governor Simcoe visited this spot, where McGregor's Creek flows into the Thames River, and named it "Chatham." This 1930s *Windsor Star* photograph shows beams which had been placed between two breakwaters to prevent the banks from eroding or caving in.

Central School was originally established in 1832 as Chatham's first publicly funded school. The building behind the rows of students was the third school building, and was erected in 1896. At one time Central was the largest Ontario public school not located in Toronto.

This impressive post office and customs building was built in 1884 at the southwest corner of King and Fourth streets, at a cost of $35,000—a high sum in those days. The building was demolished in 1957.

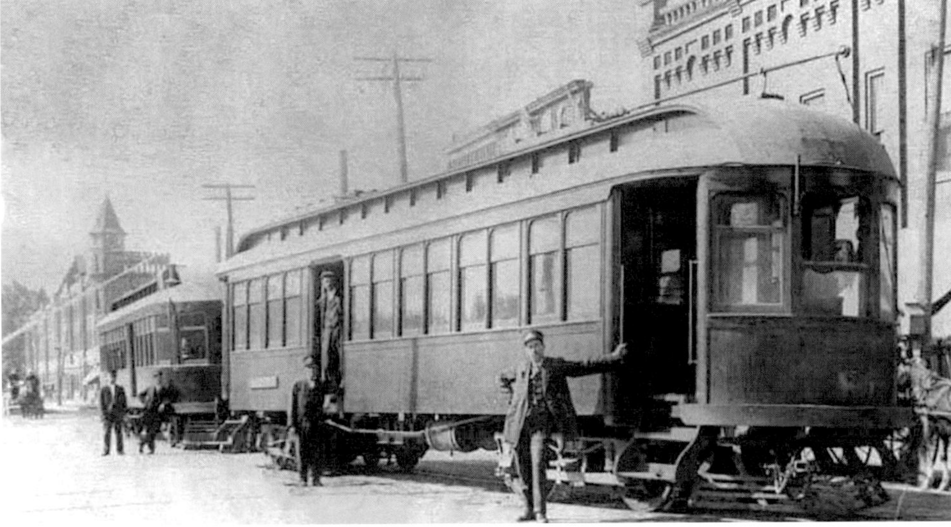

Starting in 1885, the Chatham Street Railway—which consisted of four horse-drawn streetcars running on a track down the middle of the street—travelled between the Erie and Huron railway depot on King Street E. and the Grand Trunk station on the southern outskirts of the town. The fare was five cents, one way.

It's hard to believe that the Orr house seen in this picture is now considered to be in the centre of Chatham. Riverview Gardens, once St. Joseph's Hospital, now stands to the right of this house, and beyond it, King Street W. continues for several more blocks. This early photograph is one of several in this book taken by Grace Sandys.

The interior of St. Joseph's Church in Chatham is seen here festooned in honour of a memorial service for Pope Leo XIII in 1903.

On December 12, 1882, the Chatham Manufacturing Company started building farm wagons on Head Street E. on the D.R. Van Allen property. Formerly a shipbuilding outfit, the "wagon works" continued to expand until it was purchased by the International Harvester Company in 1910.

The cannon in Tecumseh Park came to Chatham in 1902 but was a relic of the War of 1812. The large commercial building seen in the centre background is on Thames Street, across the Thames River from the park. The building on the left, of which only the back is showing, is probably the old Barracks building, which had been cut up in sections and moved across the river ice in the winter of 1879-80.

This postcard shows the forks of the Thames, where they meet McGregor's Creek, behind the new iron Fifth Street bridge, which opened in 1885. Three wooden bridges superseded this bridge, including one that was washed away in the flood of March 12, 1868. At that time, three citizens courageously got themselves onto the bridge as it was floating down the river and carefully steered it through the open Third Street bridge, so that the town would not be without both bridges.

This 1895 portrait was labelled "the ten most beautiful women in Chatham" and demonstrates the (male-imposed) ideal of "beauty" for the Victorian woman.

This well-known photograph shows very clearly what "the Forks" of the Thames River and McGregor's Creek looked like in the early days before Tecumseh Park had been laid out. This is still military ground, and here, the 24th Battalion, the Kents, is set up for muster days. Visible in the centre distance is T.H. Taylor's house, which later became the Hotel Sanita, Chatham Vocational School, and finally the Chatham Cultural Centre.

All three Richardsonian Romanesque buildings—Harrison Hall, First Presbyterian, and Central School—located at the intersection of Wellington, Fifth, Sixth, and Centre Streets were designed by T.J. Rutley and built in the 1890s. Pictured here are First Presbyterian Church, at right, which opened on July 1, 1895, and Central School, seen at left, which opened in 1896.

Harrison Hall, the home of municipal and county offices, is visible here at Sixth and Wellington streets. The house at left was the home and office of Dr. Richard Charteris, the first of three successive doctors by that name to serve in Chatham. Central School is also visible.

The County of Kent received separate jurisdiction from Essex County on July 18, 1847. The new capital, Chatham, soon received a county courthouse and jail, seen here in 1850. Among the stonemasons who worked on the building was a young Alexander Mackenzie, who went on to become Canada's second prime minister.

Kent Mills was originally established in 1847 by early entrepreneur Joseph Northwood. The business was taken over by Campbell, Stevens & Company, and in 1883 the original mills were destroyed by fire. By 1887 the mills were rebuilt—as seen here.

On June 7, 1939, as part of their whistle-stop tour of Canada, King George VI and his wife Margaret visited Chatham, ever so briefly. They didn't even disembark their special locomotive, but waved from the rear viewing platform to the thousands of people who came to see them as the train moved slowly through the city.

Formed in 1883 by R.E. Gosnell, the editor of the *Chatham Planet*, the Macaulay Club would become the oldest independent debating club in Canada. A Valentine's Day banquet and summer picnic soon became established events in the Macaulay Club schedule. The club remains today, albeit mainly inactive.

Dating back to 1931, Maple City Gas was a local landmark on the corner of Wellington and Harvey streets opposite the back of the market. First owned by Peter Gilbert, the downtown fixture stayed in the family for three generations, remaining open until the 1970s.

In the 1800s, the Chatham Livery was located on Sixth Street, right at the entrance to the footbridge into Tecumseh Park.

At one time Chatham's largest building, the malting house of Howard and Northwood flourished in the 1870s at King Street W., between First and Lacroix Streets. The malting operations could handle 100,000 bushels of grain and needed twenty employees to keep things going.

This group photo of the officers of the Kent Regiment—called the 24th during First World War—was taken outside the Armouries in Tecumseh Park in 1931. The 24th never actually served overseas as a regiment; instead it trained recruits, who then joined other regiments in the war.

The William McKeough house was built in 1878 and was named "Summerlands." By 1925, it was a funeral home called the Stephen (later, Stephen-Alexander) Funeral Home. The property today houses the Alexander-Houle Funeral Home but the original McKeough house succumbed to fire in 2009.

The Chatham, Wallaceburg and Lake Erie electric railroad was beset with problems almost from its inception. It began as a passenger line, but there wasn't a large enough passenger base and the automobile became increasingly popular after the First World War. As this picture taken on St. Clair Street shows, the trains began carrying freight, especially sugar beets during the fall harvest. However, with the heavier loads, the Third Street Bridge began to falter and the CW&LE was forced into bankruptcy.

The first references to hockey in Chatham newspapers occurred in the 1890s and included mentions of a ladies team. Hockey was being played in outdoor skating rinks, like the one outside the Armouries in Tecumseh Park, for many years before any arenas were built.

In 1892, the Waterworks system, including the water tower on Grand Avenue shown here, was finally complete. Unfortunately, the Thames water was often full of silt, causing problems until town engineer, Edwin Basset Jones, suggested a sedimentation basin.

Children enjoy the pool at Stirling Park in July 1929.

Built in 1890 on the southwest corner of Wellington and William streets, the carriage works of William Gray & Sons eventually ran all the way to Park Street and employed more than 400 people, with an output of more than 15,000 carriages each year, making them the largest carriage maker in Canada at the time.

Robert Gray and his son, William Murray, took an interest in the early car industry. In 1915, they formed a partnership with Dallas Dort of Flint, Michigan, who was already building very popular cars in the U.S. Together they developed the Gray-Dort, which took off almost immediately and was advertised as "the class of the light car field."

Robert Gray's wife, Haldane, acquired this electric car in 1920 and drove it for the rest of her life. Even though her husband owned Gray-Dort, Haldane drove this Detroit Electric car and was a familiar sight around the city of Chatham for many years. During the Second World War, she would joke that she didn't need gasoline ration coupons.

At the height of Gray-Dort's success, the company's main manufacturing plant, pictured here, was located at the southwest corner of William and Wellington streets in Chatham. The company also had a plant on Colborne Street and at the corner of St. Clair and Dover streets, as well as a showroom at the northeast corner of King and William streets and the Employees Club (the former Queen Street School) at the northwest corner of Queen and Park streets. Gray-Dort had one other factory, in Winnipeg.

An early assembly line at Gray-Dort Motors Ltd. in Chatham. The assembly line was used on a mass scale and perfected, of course, by Henry Ford.

In the days before automation, workers like these men in the machine shop (at left) and paint department (at right) in the Gray-Dort factory did the dirty, back-breaking labour of the auto industry. The painters are giving the metal bodies the shiny, colourful finish common to all Gray-Dort vehicles that arrived in the showroom.

The finished product is carefully inspected before leaving the Gray-Dort factory in Chatham.

Located on Victoria Avenue, right next to Blessed Sacrament School, this house was built by C.D. Sulman, Canada's youngest mayor when he was first elected in Chatham in 1925, being still in his twenties. He remained in public service for much of his life. His parents, who owned Sulman's Beehive on the southeast corner of King and Sixth streets, were world travelers and are famous for donating the Egyptian mummy to the Chatham-Kent Museum.

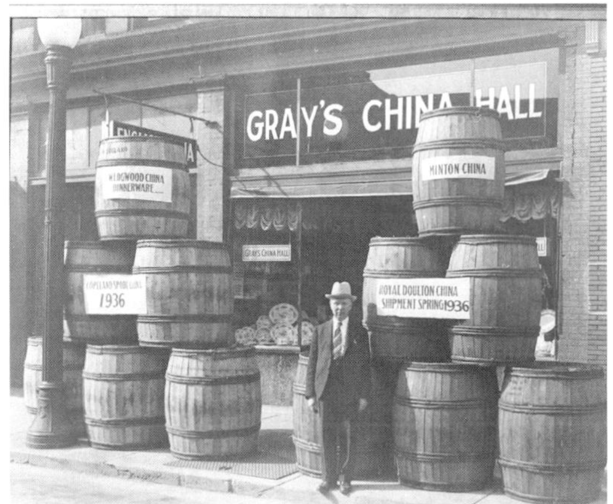

By the time this photograph was taken in 1936, Gray's China Hall had been open for business on King Street for thirty-four years. When they opened on October 25, 1902, the first day's receipts totalled $3.75. The Grays sold not only china but McClary stoves, coal-oil lamps, and dozens of other novelties. They are still in business today.

In May 1937, around 200 students from Chatham Vocational School took part in an annual inspection of the cadet corps by A.T. Brown of London, Ontario, at the Armouries. This photo, taken next to the Bandshell in Tecumseh Park just outside the Armouries, shows the CVS Cadet officers.

At their annual meeting in March 1946, the Canadian Club chapter in Chatham heard a speech from an MP from Saskatchewan, who made a strong plea for a United Nations Organization. That MP, John Diefenbaker, seen here at far left, would go on to become Prime Minister of Canada in 1957.

This photo from 1908 purports to be the O'Brien Brothers' tobacco "plantation," which it refers to "one of the largest on the continent"—likely an exaggeration.

King Street W., 1922. This postcard shows the western end of the downtown, with the Eberts building (first on right) and further down, also on the north or river side of the street, the Brisco Hotel, which was originally Scane's Opera House.

After the First World War, local butcher Jack Beardall began to experiment with amateur radio. In 1928, a commercial licence was granted to CFCO (Coming From Chatham Ontario) and the following year the station was moved from Beardall's home on Park Avenue W. to the mezzanine of the William Pitt Hotel. By 1929, the Western Ontario Better Radio Club, with Beardall at the helm, was the largest club of its type in Canada with 3000 members.

Employees from Chatham Hydro Company stand with a display in front of a large cooking class in March 1933. Their display boasts: "Hydro - Serves You Best," and "Hydro: The Clean […] Servant."

These boys, all of them seven or eight years old, are getting set to run the 100-yard dash at the annual St. Joseph Separate School field day in June 1948.

This fire on December 27, 1948, destroyed Weaver Industries on Richmond Street and took the life of Captain George H. Hill. He is the only firefighter to have died in service in Chatham. His funeral was held on the same day that would have been his son William's first day with the Chatham Fire Department.

The Union Gas Company on Fifth Street, July 19, 1950. At this time, Colonel Tom Weir, the general manager, announced that two additional storeys would be soon be added to the building.

This photograph of the Chatham Kiltie Band was taken outside of the Armouries in 1928.

A row of residential homes in Colborne Street, 1930s. McGregor's Creek runs behind these houses.

This rear view of homes in the 1930s illustrates the challenges faced by Chatham residents during the Great Depression. Many homes have outhouses and other outbuildings where chickens or other small livestock were kept.

Famous novelist Arthur Stringer was born in Chatham in 1874 and attended school here before moving to New York. He later wrote more than fifty best-selling novels, as well as screenplays, poetry, and a biography.

After Gray-Dort closed for business, Robert Gray's son, William Murray, established Colonial Traders, which he ran until the end of the Second World War. Then, instead of retiring, he became Chatham's Industrial Commissioner. Chatham was named "City of the Year" in 1947 by the *Financial Post*, and Bill Gray was named "Mr. Chatham." This photograph of Bill Gray's travel trailer—which he used for both business and pleasure—was taken outside Avenel, the Grey home.

Songwriter Geoffrey O'Hara was born in Chatham in 1882, the youngest son of an important lawyer in town, Robert O'Hara. As a child, he sang and played the organ at Holy Trinity Anglican Church. Geoffery moved to New York in 1904 but often returned to Chatham—including this visit in 1947. In this *Chatham Daily News* photo, he shows off his most famous composition, the song "K-K-Katy."

Founded by John A. Hoon in 1856, the Hoon's Bottling Company was in business until 1977. Hoon's ginger beer was a local favourite.

The first excursion steamer, built for the Chatham Navigation Company in 1888, named *The City of Chatham*, made the run from its home dock, the Rankin Dock in Chatham, down the Thames, into Lake St. Clair, and through to Detroit, daily. The boat could hold 800 people. Here it is sailing past Emma Street, in north Chatham, on its way down river in 1910, near the end of its days on the Thames.

James Couzens was born on August 26, 1872, in a row house (pictured here) near the corner of Grand Avenue and Elizabeth Street. As a boy, he held a number of jobs: pumping the organ at St. Andrew's Presbyterian Church, tending the town's lamps, and selling soap from his father's factory. He attended Canada Business College and moved to Detroit in 1890 to work for none other than Henry Ford.

James Couzens, at left, with his employer, Henry Ford. Under Couzens, the Ford Motor Company experienced phenomenal financial growth. Couzens was famous for instituting several key labour policies, including the five-dollar day and the eight-hours work day.

FIFTEEN CENTS

TIME

The Weekly News-Magazine

VOL. 1, NO. 20 — SENATOR JAMES C. COUZENS — JULY 16, 1923

After his time at Ford, Couzens joined public service—first as Supervisor of Police Services in Detroit (1916-18), then Mayor of Detroit (1919-22), and finally as a U.S. Senator (1922-36). Here, he graces the cover of *Time* magazine.

James Adams and his wife Margaret established a grocery at the corner of Raleigh and Cross streets around 1914 before building the Adams block at the corner of Queen and Centre streets in 1916. By 1950, it was Adam's Confectionery, as seen here.

Built on the east side of Sixth Street in 1881, this firehall housed Chatham's first professional firefighters. Its central location allowed the department to respond quickly to fires, and the fire tower pictured here, circa 1910, helped firefighters to spot blazes before they got out of control.

The Chatham, Wallaceburg and Lake Erie Powerhouse, shown here circa 1910, was located near the north-east corner of King and Third streets in downtown Chatham. It powered the electric railroad lines until a dramatic explosion destroyed the rear of the building and killed Charles Davies, an engineer employed by the Chatham Gas Company.

In 1934, the Chatham Coloured All-Stars beat stiff competition from Sarnia, Welland, Milton, and Penetang to win the Ontario Baseball Association Intermediate Championship. In an era of open and unashamed prejudice, the victory was a remarkable achievement.

This photograph from October 22, 1932, shows two men assembling machinery at the Soy Bean Oil and Meal Co-operative Company of Canada Ltd. of Chatham, located at Colbourne and Adelaide streets. Some 700 farmers gained membership with a $50 share, allowing them to sell beans to the company. However, the crushing plant underperformed and was dogged by scandal until its manager, Mr. Biles, disappeared with $7,000 in company funds. The plant was shuttered in 1935.

This Wolfe Studios photograph shows Queen Mary's Public School on Queen Street in Chatham. Alfred A. Naylor came to Queen Mary in 1919 and served as principle for thirty-four years—more than a third of a century!

This photograph of Harrison Hall appeared in the *Windsor Star* on June 30, 1948, along with an article detailing Kent County's search for a new county building. Built as shared municipal-county offices, Harrison Hall had reverted to the City of Chatham as its second city hall.

An ice storm blanketed this Chatham neighbourhood in January 1947. Winter snow and ice storms are common in this area, which is situated between Lake Erie and Lake St. Clair.

The Chatham Hotel is seen here in this photograph by Wolfe Studios, shortly after the hotel opened its doors on Fifth Street on January 13, 1934. Across the street is the Union Gas Building—the utility company's second home in Chatham—which was built in 1928. The Victoria building also sits on the southwest corner of King and Fifth streets, across from the Eberts building. Built in 1855, the Eberts building was one of the oldest in the downtown. Also visible on the east side of that intersection are both the Royal Bank of Canada and the Bank of Montreal.

Memorial Square, at the north end of Sixth Street, is decorated for the holiday season in this photograph taken on December 21, 1931. The cenotaph, commemorating Kent County's fallen from the Great War, was the result of the efforts of private citizens and the 24th Kent Regiment Chapter of the IODE. It was unveiled in 1923.

Bell Telephone Co., Sixth Street, Chatham. In 1900, Bell and the City of Chatham were embroiled in a case heard by the Supreme Court of Canada. The City was being sued for negligence by Mary Louisa Atkinson over the placement of a telephone pole on King Street. Bell was a third party, brought in to indemnify the City. While the City ended up winning the appeal, they did have to pay Bell's legal fees for trying to make the company liable if they lost.

Shovelling snow on Sixth Street, 1947. Behind the men, the William Pitt Hotel, Imperial Bank of Canada, the Chatham Cenotaph, Tamblyn Drug Store, the Canadian Bank of Commerce, and Sulman's Beehive are visible, from left to right. This end of Sixth Street no longer exists; the downtown mall was built there in 1980.

Lenover's Meat Market, located at 525 Park Avenue E. in Chatham, opened for business in 1938. Pictured here are the first generation of Lenover Brothers. The people of Chatham are still getting their fresh meat from Lenover's today.

This *Windsor Star* photograph from October 14, 1949, shows the brand-new Chatham Memorial Arena on the night the stadium hosted its inaugural game, the Chatham Maroons against the Windsor Spitfires. The arena took ten years to build and cost $233,000. The *Star* caption puts it best: "A decade is a long time to wait for hockey in your hometown."

Spectators line Chatham's Fifth Street Bridge looking in awe at the high waters levels during the flood of 1947.

INDEX

ACKNOWLEDGEMENTS

Kent County, like many other counties, has several small communities that once thrived along roads, waterways, and railroads. Each has something unique about it, but together they tell the tale of the emerging and then prosperous southland of Canada. For many people, it is still galling to think that their community's identity has been lost within the greater Municipality of Chatham-Kent, but rest assured, its past is still secure.

One of the most reassuring discoveries we made in the course of researching this book was the existence of many local heritage organizations. Without fail, these organizations made us feel welcome, and they opened their treasures to us. They kindly lent us pictures or scanned them for us. They looked for details that we needed to complete stories. They gave us their expertise, and the strength of this book really rests on their shoulders. They proudly showed us their collection, but they also worried that their presence wasn't well known in the community, and that in the future they might be lost. We hope that our readers, no matter where they are from, will join the group that is protecting their local heritage collection. They can use you.

In that regard, we would like to individually acknowledge these organizations, and the people that helped us. The Blenheim Heritage House was very helpful, in particular Mary Lou Little, Nancy Foulis, and Stan Uher, whose wonderful calendars provided many of the photos of Blenheim in this book. The Mary Webb Centre is the heritage centre for the Highgate area, and Mary Eberle was very generous with both her time and her resources. Thamesville's Townhall Museum is a treasure trove for that community, and many thanks to Chris Crawford, who provided several files of pictures for us to choose from. The Lanoue House in Tilbury is an amazing reconstruction of an early Francophone dwelling, and several people there were very helpful. Thanks in particular to Gary St. Jean, Margaret Mailloux, and Liz and Jim Garlick. The Wallaceburg and District Museum is an amazing place, with a dedicated volunteer group to help run it. Particular thanks go to Ariel Mann, who is a loving custodian of her late husband's extensive collection, as well as the curator Andrea Lalonde. In Wheatley, the Friendship Centre is another beehive of activity, with many important pictures and documents catalogued in their heritage rooms. Thanks go to Heather Vannieuwenburg, Pat Churchill, and Marcia Kennedy, who took time, even though they were closed for the summer, to help us find and scan pictures. Down in Windsor, we must thank the *Windsor Star* and managing editor Craig Pearson for opening up their archive and letting us publish select, rare newspaper photographs from their collection.

Where organizations do not exist, many individuals helped us instead. Bothwell's Marion Matt is a one-woman heritage industry. She generously opened up the picture files from her book, *Life in a Boomtown*, many of which you will see in our Bothwell section. In Dresden, Jim Burns kindly lent us his photo and postcard albums, which form the bulk of the Dresden section. For Bradley Farms, Dean Bradley graciously gave us several family photos. Our Merlin section would be non-existent if it weren't for Sue Marshall, with help from Les Mancell. In Erieau, Jeff Vidler collects precious memories, as well as photographs. Susan and Tom Hebblethwaite kindly helped us with the New Scotland pictures, as did Jim Burgess with Kent Bridge, and Bill Stephens with Rondeau. Thanks also to Jerry Hind for help with information about the Japanese internment camps; to Jim Purdy for his advice regarding Chatham military photos; to John Jordan for the picture and research from Tilbury East; and to Ron and Bonnie VanRabaeys for help in Thamesville. Thanks also to Kate Clendenning from Raglan and Robert Thomas from Wheatley.

Many small villages are present here in sketches by Elsie Thoonen, who, regretfully, passed away recently. Elsie's sketches and research into many of Kent's forgotten hamlets were invaluable to us, and we encourage you to look at her books as well. Thanks to Perry and Pat Dolsen for allowing us to photograph their painting of Howard Bridge. Thanks so much also to our friend Sheila Gibbs, who helped us immensely with researching some of the *Chatham Daily News* photos which found their way into this book. We also, of course, must thank the staff at the Chatham Public Library.

Last, and certainly not least, we want to thank the Chatham-Kent Museum, our official partners on this project. With sincere thanks, in particular, to curators Stephanie Saunders and Lydia Burggraaf, who opened up the archives for us and had abundant patience as we looked for just the right photographs to make this book come to life.

For all of these individuals and organizations, once again, we give hearty thanks. We also would be remiss if we didn't mention our wonderful editor, Sharon Hanna: she has been unflaggingly positive, and her patience in the face of any problems or complaints we might have had has been an inspiration to us. Any errors or omissions are ours alone. Thanks, finally, to our families, for putting up with us while we were engaged in this "summer of the book."

We hope this book gives you an appreciation for the dedication and perseverance that our forebears brought to their communities. It is bittersweet to realize how much they did, and to see so much of it now gone.

But not completely—there are always the pictures and the stories.

—Jim and Lisa Gilbert, 2018

PHOTO CREDITS

A.E.D. MacKenzie, *Baldoon—Lord Selkirk's Settlement in Upper Canada,* 1978, Phelps Publishing Co., London, Ontario—67

Ariel Mann, from the Al Mann collection in the Wallaceburg and District Museum—21, 48–63, 68

Authors' Private Collection—67, 98, 100, 102, 114, 116, 119, 123, 131, 132, 138, 156, 160, 184

Buxton National Historic Site and Museum—99, 123, 124, 125, 126, 127

Centennial Book Committee, *Eglise St. Philippe Church, 1886-1986 Centennial*—68, 69

Chatham-Kent Museum—14, 19, 20, 21, 36, 37, 75, 77–79, 86, 111, 128, 130, 133, 155, 157–160, 162–178, 181–193

Chris Crawford—Old Town Hall Museum, Thamesville—39–47

Dean Bradley—74, 76, 79, 132

Don Spearman, *Landmarks from the Past – A Pictorial History of Dresden and Area,* Stephen Lance Enterprises, 1991, Dresden, Ont.—27, 38, 47

Elsie Thoonen—69, 138

Gordon H. Shaw, H.S. Feagan, eds., *Ridgetown Album—Historical Homes and Landmarks, 1875-1975, Centennial Edition*, Ridgetown Dominion Press, Ridgetown, Ont.—93–97

Historical Atlas of Essex and Kent County, 1881—16, 19, 30, 64, 80, 120, 152, 169

Historical Society of Blenheim and District—83–92, 107

Jerry Hind—77, 118

Jim Burgess—39, 40, 187

Jim Burns—27–38

Jim Vidler, *Erieau Then and Now—A Chronological History of Erieau, With Pictures.*,2012—102–106

John Jordan—147

John Rhodes, *Come Walking and Leave Early—A Pictorial History of the Chatham, Wallaceburg and Lake Erie Electric Railway Co.*, Mercury Press, Chatham, Ontario, 1989—131

Marg Eberle and the Mary Webb Centre, Highgate—107–110, 117

Marion Matt—19–27

Marjorie Giddis, ed., *As the Story is Told—A History of Morpeth and Community,* 1986, Dominion Press Ltd., Ridgetown, Ont.—97, 98

Pain Court 150—70–74

Perry and Pat Dolsen—115

Rob Kerr, Randy Moore, *Duart... It's About Time,* 2000, Print Three Publishing Co., Toronto, Ont.—110, 112

S.S.#2 Orford Township Reunion Committee, *Palmyra Memories*, 2002— 113

Southwestern Ontario Digital Archive—50, 53, 57, 59, 60, 129, 131, 136

Sue Marshall—134, 135, 137

Tilbury and District Historical Society—Lanoue House Collection—131, 138, 139, 141–148

Tom and Susan Hebblethwaite—116, 118

Victor Lauriston, *Blue Flame of Service—A History of Union Gas Company and the Natural Gas Industry in Southwestern Ontario*, 1961, Union Gas Company of Canada Ltd., Chatham, Ont.—137, 140

Wheatley Friendship Centre Collection—146, 147, 149, 150, 151

William Stephen, *Rondeau Forever—A Family Tradition*, 2009—99–101

Windsor Star—52, 55, 63, 128, 161, 169, 171, 190, 192, 193

ABOUT THE AUTHORS

Jim and Lisa Gilbert have been bringing local history to life for almost forty years in Chatham-Kent. They have won local, regional, national, and international awards for their radio shows, newspaper columns, historical presentations, and other heritage programming. Their living history festival—Heritage Days: The Faire at the Forks—was the largest of its kind in Canada. They spearheaded a campaign to bring greater recognition to the Tecumseh Monument. They have served on committees, boards, and organizations throughout their lives which help to bring recognition to Chatham-Kent's rich history. They hope this book does that as well.